Editor's Introduction
The Portrait Issue

This month we take you on a round-the-world trip by way of France, Nepal and New Zealand, focusing on different approaches to portraiture and representation, from *The Feminist Memory Project* initiated by Photo Kathmandu, to a notorious Kiwi gang, and a collaboration between the grande dame of Gallic cinema, Agnès Varda, and street artist, JR.

But we begin in Cradley Heath, the West Midlands town where Richard Billingham grew up and later photographed his chaotic family home, going on to publish one of the landmark photobooks of the 1990s, *Ray's a Laugh*. Now he's returned to make his debut feature film, *Ray & Liz*, an attempt to "provide a backstory for the photographs". We visited the set in January, and fresh from it winning the Special Mention award at the Locarno Film Festival, we bring you Billingham's thoughts on translating a personal – and controversial – portrait of his family to the cinema.

We also present a selection of the 100 pictures picked for the third edition of Portrait Of Britain, which takes over high streets, shopping centres and major transport hubs across the country throughout September, thanks to our collaboration with JCDecaux. This year we've also partnered with Hoxton Mini Press to present a wider edit of 200 pictures, now available as a hardback book.

We are also announcing our most ambitious project to date, with the launch of Portrait Of Humanity, a collaboration between our publisher, 1854 Media, and Magnum Photos. Look out for news at bjp-online.com, including details on how to take part, and our partnerships with international photofestivals, who will stage a series of exhibitions of the winners across three continents.

Simon Bainbridge
Editor

THE INTERNATIONAL ART FAIR FOR PHOTOGRAPHY

PARIS PHOTO

8.11 NOV 2018
GRAND PALAIS

FAIR SECTORS
GALLERIES / BOOK / PRISMES / CURIOSA / FILM

PROGRAMMING
EXHIBITIONS / CONVERSATIONS / AWARDS / BOOK SIGNINGS

Official Partners

 Reed Expositions   WWW.PARISPHOTO.COM   J.P.Morgan

Featured

50–67
Portrait Of Britain
Returning to JCDecaux billboards across the UK (and now a 336-page book), the country's largest public photography exhibition brings together 200 portraits of the nation. We highlight the pick of the winning entries.

68–80
Chapter and verse
Jono Rotman spent a decade photographing the tattooed faces and insignia of the Mongrel Mob, one of New Zealand's most notorious gangs. The portraits are compelling but at odds with society's perception of them.

38–43
Back home
Richard Billingham came to fame with *Ray's a Laugh*, an unflinching portrayal of his family life in the Midlands. Now he's returned there to make *Ray & Liz*, a personal film of his "lived experience". We visit the set of his cinematic debut.

44–49
On the road
Teaming up for a unique road trip, artist JR and nouvelle vague pioneer Agnès Varda travelled across France finding soul in its declining villages. The result is *Faces Places*, an intimate film that may be Varda's last.

Index

Projects

23 Maria Sturm visits the Lumbee Tribe of North Carolina for her work looking at Native American identity.

26 An assignment in Toulon finds Daragh Soden addressing issues of history and contemporary extremism.

28 Juan Jose Barboza-Gubo & Andrew Mroczek offer an empowering vision for the transgender community of Lima, Peru.

32 Marzena Skubatz documents the life of a lone weather-watcher in the dramatic landscapes of Iceland.

Features

38 A film by Richard Billingham revisits his orderless family life in Black Country public housing, the place that inspired his original photography.

44 As she reaches her 90th birthday, legendary filmmaker Agnès Varda teams up with street artist JR for a special French travelogue.

50 The return of Portrait Of Britain, the UK's largest state-of-the-nation exhibition.

68 Jono Rotman gets up close with one of New Zealand's most infamous gangs for his series, *Mongrelism*.

Intelligence

83 Looking at the genesis and ethos of Photo Kathmandu as it prepares for its third edition.

88 This month our Creative Brief is Emily Keegin, photo director of *The Fader*.

90 Can a smartphone compete with a professional camera? We test the Huawei P20 Pro and Samsung Galaxy S9+ to find out.

Endframe

98 The archives of *Ebony* and *Jet* magazines are utilised for *The Black Image Corporation*, a celebration of black beauty in the 1940s and beyond.

Agenda

13 London's Barbican presents *Modern Couples*, a far-reaching exhibition exploring the role of romance and relationships in creative endeavour.

16 A new show at The Met Breuer in New York considers photography's role in conspiracy theories.

18 Stephen McLaren's book *The Crash* takes a critical perspective on the 2008 financial meltdown in the Square Mile.

20 Any Answers: Ohio-born Todd Hido on the search for home, the influence of Alfred Hitchcock and making "paper movies".

20 – 21

28 – 31

90 – 93

OPPORTUNITY

機————遇

CALL FOR
PROPOSALS
AND
SUBMISSIONS

The WMA Commission & WMA Masters invite entries for proposals and image submissions from artists and photographers from both Hong Kong and the international community. Entries must relate to the theme, "Opportunity", and be relevant to Hong Kong.

WMA Commission 2018/19
Submission Deadline
14 September 2018, 23:59 HKT (GMT+8:00)

WMA Masters 2018/19
Submission Deadline
28 September 2018, 23:59 HKT (GMT+8:00)

WMA.HK | **f** WMA | ⊙ WMA_HK

Portrait of Humanity

There is more
that unites us
than sets us apart.

**Calling all photographers
to show us the world
through their eyes**

Open for entries: 06 September 2018
www.portraitofhumanity.co

Image: © Alessandra Sanguinetti / Magnum Photos

1854

Contributors

The Portrait Issue
October 2018
Issue 7876, Volume 165

Cover
Richard © Gavin Li.
Back cover
Abdel © David Cantor.

Stephen McLaren

Starting out as a TV producer and director, McLaren has turned his focus to photography, writing and curating since 2005. He is the co-author of the bestseller, *Street Photography Now,* with Sophie Howarth, and has curated exhibitions in the UK and abroad. We speak to him about his new book, *The Crash*, 10 years on from the 2008 financial crisis. "I was naive and thought it would last a year or so," he says. "In actuality, a credit crunch became a financial crisis, became a recession, which led to austerity and, ultimately, Brexit. I don't deal directly with those political ramifications in the book but the clues are there in some pictures." Based in Los Angeles, he is currently working on an American road-trip series, *Drive Lincoln.* "It keeps me sane while Trump is doing his crazy worst in these parts," he says.

stephenmclaren.co.uk

Allie Haeusslein

Associate director of Pier 24 in San Francisco, Haeusslein's writing has appeared in publications such as *Aperture, ART21* magazine and *Foam* magazine, and she contributed one of the two essays for Chris McCaw's 2012 monograph, *Sunburn*. For this issue, she interviewed Jono Rotman on his controversial series, *Mongrelism*. "It is obvious he has spent a great deal of time grappling with the project's meaning, the photographer's role and responsibilities, and his relationship to his native New Zealand," she says of Rotman. Overwhelmed by the series at first, this quickly turned to curiosity. She says: "Once I saw Jono's photographs in person, I was in awe of the work's incredible presence and nuance."

pier24.org

Tom Seymour

Seymour is the former online editor of *BJP* and now a freelance journalist, writing for *The Guardian*, *The Telegraph*, *Financial Times*, *FT Weekend Magazine*, *New Statesman*, *Wired*, *Wallpaper** and the BBC, among others. He recently produced a photography exhibition for the National Portrait Gallery, and hosts artist talks for Sotheby's. He spoke to renowned director Agnès Varda about her new film, *Faces Places*. And he believes Varda "should be regarded as one of the nouvelle vague's most distinctive and powerful voices, yet she's always been overlooked. It was fantastic to see how stills photography has played such an integral part in her practice as a filmmaker. She's a humble woman, happy to let others take the limelight. It was a pleasure to speak to her – any photographer or filmmaker should seek guidance and inspiration from her 60-plus years of creativity."

@tomseymour

Editor
Simon Bainbridge

Digital Editor
Diane Smyth

Assistant Editor
Izabela Radwanska Zhang

Creative Director
Mick Moore

Senior Designer
Nicky Brown

Chief Sub-Editor
Kathy Ball

Contributors
Daniel Boetker-Smith, Laurence Butet-Roch, Federica Chiocchetti, Jörg Colberg, Joanna Cresswell, Lucy Davies, Damien Demolder, Martin Evening, Marc Feustel, Gem Fletcher, Michael Grieve, Peter Hamilton, Lauren Heinz, Allie Haeusslein, Charlotte Jansen, David Kilpatrick, Cat Lachowskyj, Stephen McLaren, Donatella Montrone, Gemma Padley, Colin Pantall, Juan Peces, Matthew Ponsford, Aaron Schuman, Rachel Segal Hamilton, Tom Seymour, Maisie Skidmore, Nina Strand, Shana Ting Lipton, Erik Vroons, Paul Wombell, Sophie Wright, Alice Zoo

Editorial Enquiries
editorial@bjphoto.co.uk

Sales Enquiries
sales@1854.media

Head of Agency
Pax Zoega

Head of Client Services
Ameena Rojee

Operations & Analytics Director
Marc Ghione

**Creative Development
& Awards Director**
Melanie Philippe

Creative Campaign Manager
Harry Rose

CTO
Tom Royal

Chief Executive Officer
Marc Hartog

Subscription Enquiries
020 7993 2243
subscriptions@1854.media

Distribution & Marketing Enquiries
marketing@1854.media

1854 Media
9th Floor, Import Building,
2 Clove Crescent, London E14 2BE
020 7193 2625

Distributed by Seymour Distribution Ltd

Printed by Stephens & George Ltd

ISSN: 0007-1196

*Published by 1854 Media Ltd
© 1854 Media Ltd, 34a Watling Street, Radlett, Herts, WD7 7NN.
UK Company No: 8361351.*

RONIN-S

DARE TO MOVE

Video is picture in motion. Soon, your motion is video in perfect pictures!
Thanks to the compact design, ease of use and compatibility of the new Ronin-S,
combined with our vast experience in image stabilization, any photographer
is now able to shoot smooth videos on-the-go. So, do you dare to see what you
and your camera are truly capable of?

Move here for all details: **dji.com/ronin-s**

British Journal of Photography has collaborated
with Hoxton Mini Press on this year's Portrait Of Britain
to present a 336-page hardback book featuring all
200 shortlisted photographs and an introduction by Will Self

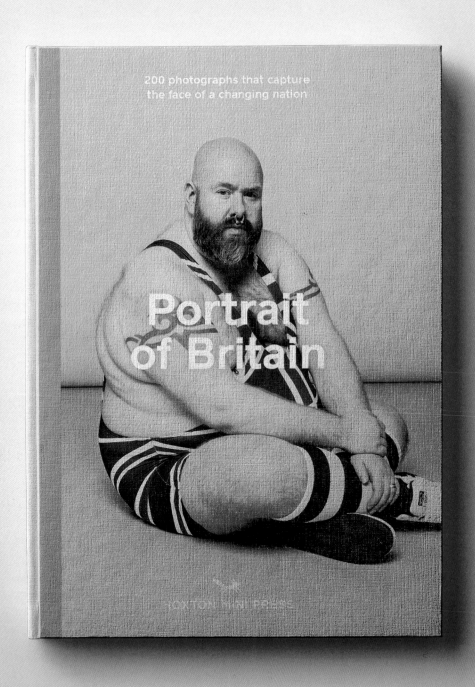

An expansive exhibition at the Barbican interrogates the power of romantic relationships to propel artistic output

Modern Couples

Words by Maisie Skidmore

"From the 1890s through to just after the Second World War, modern artist couples forged new ways of making art and of living and loving," Jane Alison, head of visual arts at London's Barbican, says. She's putting the final touches to *Modern Couples: Art, Intimacy and the Avant-garde* – a mammoth endeavour that examines how the work of individual artists and writers was shaped by the relationships they embarked on with each other. The show spans painting, sculpture, literature, dance, music, architecture and photography, and while it includes some of the resulting artworks, it also has ephemera – personal photographs, gifts and love letters – on display.

Modern Couples (10 October to 27 January) is far from a cursory look at the history of art's favourite romantic pairings. Certainly the likes of Virginia Woolf and Vita Sackville-West, or Frida Kahlo and Diego Rivera, have their part to play here, but so do lesser-known affiliations, from Claude Cahun and Marcel Moore to George Platt Lynes, Monroe Wheeler and Glenway Wescott, whose enduring ménage à trois turned their travels around Europe into an intensely fruitful creative experience. One of the discoveries of the exhibition is the photographic trio of Paul Cadmus, Jared French and Margaret French, known collectively as PaJaMa [1], whose "potent images, often taken of one another, highlight the emergence of a graphic homoeroticism in the American interwar period", says the Barbican exhibition foreword.

"Ultimately it is an exhibition about modern art and modern love," says Alison, who has conceived the exhibition as a journey through a series of rooms, each dedicated to different couples, allowing visitors to immerse themselves in their shared romantic and creative encounters. Two displays focus on larger communities of artists: one devoted to surrealism's 'Chance Encounter', and the other to radical lesbian artists of the Parisian Left Bank during the 1920s and 30s. The show also seeks to interrogate anew the much-discussed

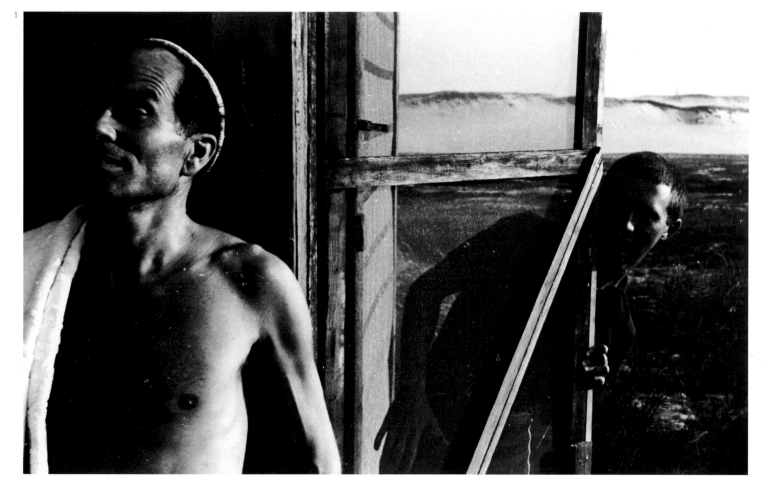

1

1   Jared French and Roberto Giannotta,
     Provincetown, 1947 © PaJaMa, courtesy
     of DC Moore Gallery, New York.

2   *Tina Reciting*, 1924 © Edward Weston,
     courtesy of Wilson Centre for Photography.

3   Dorothea Tanning and Max Ernst with
     his sculpture, Capricorn, 1947
     © John Kasnetsis.

4   Aleksandr Rodchenko and Varvara
     Stepanova descending from the airplane,
     1926, artist unknown, courtesy of the
     Rodchenko and Stepanova Archives.

artist-muse relationship. The era in question saw women fight for "and ultimately achieve an unprecedented amount of autonomy as practising artists", Alison continues – and even where they played muses, they often wielded artistic power. Take the photographs Alfred Stieglitz made over the course of his relationship with Georgia O'Keeffe, for example. "It's evident that O'Keeffe had an agency in those pictures," Alison says. "She was very actively engaged with exploring different aspects of her identity with Stieglitz, and I think he saw those photographs of her as a kind of gift to her."

Elsewhere, photographs by Gustav Klimt of his partner, muse and lifelong companion, Emilie Flöge, show an artist and his muse creating work together in order to financially support their independent pursuits. "Now, of course, we don't think of Klimt as a photographer, but he took probably the first artist-as-fashion-photographer pictures. Flöge ran a couture house, and she was also a designer and a businesswoman – and he supported that by taking photographs of her."

Alison is quick to point out that it isn't all rosy. "There are very different kinds of relationships in the exhibition – some of them lifelong, devoted, fulfilled, empowered and respectful. And others were very troubled, or tragic in some cases. At the time, it was difficult and courageous to lead these kinds of lives – they went against the norms and conventions of society." The work made by Dora Maar, the French surrealist photographer, painter and poet during her decade-long relationship with Pablo Picasso, is a case in point. "Maar was an independent, intelligent, creative artist in her own right," she says. Their story ended badly – but the opportunity to see Maar's work displayed on its own terms in the exhibition is a satisfying one nonetheless.

The show's aim ultimately is "to look at the couple as a catalyst for creative dialogue", says Alison. What *Modern Couples* seems to suggest is that if love was the catalyst, it was often the photographer's darkroom – that liminal, womb-like space – that incubated and protected creative fulfilment in its early form. **BJP**

barbican.org.uk

The role of photography as a record of truth is put under the spotlight in a new exhibition at The Met Breuer in New York exploring conspiracy theories through the decades

Everything Is Connected

Words by Cat Lachowskyj

Think about conspiracy theories and the initial topics that come to mind often occupy a realm that's beyond an everyday belief system – stories such as the Loch Ness Monster, Bigfoot or similar tales that are better contextualised as 'urban legends'. While those stories might not have much truth to offer, there are many other theories within the category that, although fantastical, contain far more fact than fiction. These include the secretive workings of those in power which lead to a mutual feeling of suspicion between the authorities, government and citizens.

What is arguably more interesting than the concepts themselves, however, is the way that some individuals compile their own investigative research on suspicious topics, creating accessible and expressive visuals soaked in data, philosophy, and their take on the truth.

From 18 September to 06 January, The Met Breuer in New York will exhibit the expansive show *Everything Is Connected: Art and Conspiracy*, featuring 70 works by 30 artists who represent an alternative to postwar and contemporary art from 1969 to 2016. The media presented in the exhibition is limitless, and includes painting, sculpture, video, installation art and, of course, photography.

"We wanted the show to start in the 1960s following the assassination of JFK, so some projects directly deal with this topic in particular, and the others branch out from there," explains the Met's curator in modern and contemporary art, Ian Alteveer. "The Kennedy assassination is the jumping-off point for everything that comes into play throughout the rest of the exhibition. We set the stage with the tension between government investigations into the murder and the public distrust of what the government claims to have uncovered."

This distrust is the foundational thread of the show, which includes works by artists such as Mark Lombardi, Jenny Holzer and Hans Haacke. Image-based artist Trevor Paglen's work will also be on view, as well as pieces by Emory Douglas, the former minister of culture in the Black Panther Party, who also designed the organisation's newspaper.

As Alteveer reels off the names of one incredible artist after another – including Sue Williams, Mike Kelley, Jim Shaw [1] and Tony Oursler – it's clear that the show is, in fact, a remarkable network of investigators who have made it their life's work to uncover the expansive web of money, power and deception that not only exists in the US, but all over the world. And while the range of topics are diverse, the uniting factor between all these artists is clear: they are addressing issues that seem speculative, despite their truth, and implementing their craft to make them into something tangible.

As a medium historically delegated as a legitimate visual record of evidence or truth,

1

1   *UFO Polaroid*, from the series
    UFO Photos, 1977 © Jim Shaw.

2   *Black Cloud*, 2008 © Sarah Anne
    Johnson, courtesy of Art Gallery of
    Ontario, Toronto.

3   Image from the video *1906*, 2003
    © Jeremy Blake, courtesy of the
    Metropolitan Museum of Art.

photography plays a particularly interesting part in conspiracy theories. We are constantly directed to photos as objects of proof, whether it's a blurred glimpse of a UFO or a group shot of dodgy politicians with members of confidential government projects. But what *Everything Is Connected* aims to highlight is that many artists use photography to talk about conspiracy in different ways, often as a critical demonstration of our reliance on the medium as some sort of ultimate truth.

"Take Sarah Charlesworth, for example," explains Alteveer. "She takes images of every newspaper printed on a particular day in 1978 depicting Italian prime minister Aldo Moro's face, removing all text from her reproductions, leaving just the images. This allows you to see the scale of the image on each different front page, confronting the way that the image is working towards telling a narrative about power and the continuity of world powers, even in moments of crisis."

Conversely, artists such as Rachel Harrison use the medium to address the fallibility of the photographic process. For Harrison's installation in the show, titled *Snake in the Grass*, the artist combines snapshots taken at Dealey Plaza – the location of Kennedy's assassination – with her own photographs of grass. "She had them printed at six different photo studios," explains Alteveer. "So you have five or six varying colours of green grass. It makes you ask: what colour is grass really? I think that's a particularly clever use of photography."

It's important to note that the work in the show doesn't extend to 2018, its cut-off point set to 2016, when America's current president was elected. "We deliberately decided not to tackle anything after 2016. I think we realised that when we look at Nixon and Watergate, and the government investigations that came out of that some 40-plus years ago, they are actually deeply connected to what's happening now. There are so many complex threads, and once you begin to pull one, all sorts of other things come out," reflects Alteveer. "I really see this project as the first of many on these kinds of phenomena. I think that once you begin to dig a little deeper – and you don't have to go far – you begin to see that everything is indeed connected." **BJP**

metmuseum.org

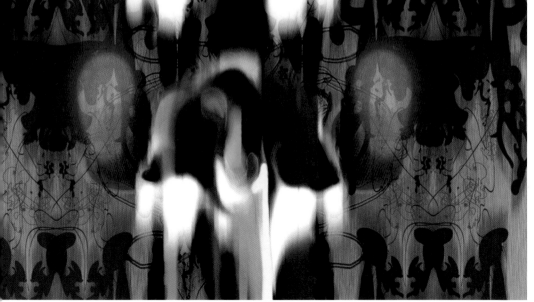

Fear and loathing in the City: Stephen McLaren recalls the financial meltdown of a decade ago in a book that warns against its 'business-as-usual' recovery

The Crash

Words by Matthew Ponsford

In early 2008, as the British bank Northern Rock and, shortly after, Lehman Brothers in the US collapsed, Stephen McLaren began making a daily journey from his home in east London to the Square Mile of the City. Embedded in Europe's financial heart, the Scottish photographer spent his days eavesdropping on bankers, arguing with hostile security guards, and trying to read stress-lined faces to understand just how bad things were about to get.

McLaren, a street photographer with a degree in economics, spent his mornings binge-reading newspapers and books, such as *Fool's Gold* by *Financial Times* journalist, Gillian Tett, making the first attempts to explain the meltdown, and why no one seemed to see it coming. But his interest was anything but academic. "I would go down there most days with a sense of burning rage," he says. "Some of the pictures, and the dark humour that's in them, come from that: not going down there dispassionate, with an 'Oh, let's see what happens' mentality. Actually going down in quite an emotional state."

McLaren's clear reading of the City – both as financial superstructure and condensed urban space – allowed him to seize spontaneous moments photographing workers against the backdrop of economic freefall. *The Crash*, published by Hoxton Mini Press, is a group portrait of bulging bodies in expensive suits, twisting and sweating to evade the consequences of the mayhem unleashed by their actions.

The caffeine-fuelled mania of the capital's uncertainty is shot with immediacy, using oblique angles and an appropriate slathering of disgust. The subjects – often unsympathetically portrayed as a collage of balding heads, contorted bodies and screwed-up faces – make up something of a surrealist anthropological study of a society characterised by moral failure.

A decade after the nadir of the financial crisis, McLaren says the events he witnessed up-close have set in motion a series of consequences that continue to evolve and have a noticeable effect. "Ten years later, I feel completely confirmed in my views that they were basically running a huge racket, one that led to the austerity programme of the Tory government, and ultimately to Brexit," he says.

In the years since, McLaren has documented how seamlessly the City returned to business-as-usual – very much unreformed. Later chapters in the book deal with heavy-handed police suppression of protests and newer crises. One image sums it up the neatest: taken in 2012, on the day when the coalition government led by David Cameron cut taxes for high earners, it shows a grinning financier in the street, barely managing to haul a giant box labelled 'Champagne'.

McLaren says *The Crash* is an important reminder to not regard these scenes as distant, "quaint times", and presents it as a piece of living history, where "the fallout is coming up with populist politicians running around wanting more chaos".

After almost five years of editing, following his departure from London to Los Angeles, McLaren says the shots he is most proud of are those made possible by him anticipating the rhythms of the City. Among them are the recurring images of burned-out employees shaving seconds off their commute by leaping over street furniture and squeezing through gaps in fences in a rodent-like scurry. Such habits have remained the same since the start of the crash when big banks, such as Royal Bank of Scotland (which reported a loss of £24.1billion for 2008, the biggest in British corporate history), faced bankruptcy.

"These people lead very solitary work lives. They go in, they probably hate their job, and they leave and depart quickly," McLaren explains. "There's very little hanging about, especially when the shit was hitting the fan. You really got the sense that people were just waiting, hoping to get out alive." **BJP**

hoxtonminipress.com

Any Answers
Todd Hido

Interview & portrait by Michael Grieve

He's best known for his cinematic gaze on night-time suburbia, coming to international attention with the publication of *House Hunting* in 2001. Since then, the Ohio-born photographer has published more than a dozen photobooks, with his next – a departure from his previous works – due this autumn

I know precisely why I have gravitated towards making work that utilises melancholy. It's me referencing my history of having an alcoholic father and a broken family as the chief reservoir for making my imagery. Instead of beating around the bush, like so many people do, I learned early on to draw from within, as that is the richest and deepest well you will ever find.

I learned from my parents mostly what not to do. However, my mother certainly taught me how to survive and persevere.

My earliest inspiration as a young photographer was Emmet Gowin. I was struck by the intense and real love that Emmet and his wife, Edith, had for each other. It inspired me to make many photographs, and pointed me in the direction of knowing that my photographs were about relationships, regardless of whether there were any people in them.

Alfred Hitchcock was a great influence. His inspiration gave me permission to make narratives that are not necessarily positive, yet they also have an obliqueness to their outcome.

It took me until graduate school to find my voice in photography. It came from melding together my love of bleaching, toning and modifying black-and-white pictures in the darkroom with my newfound opportunity to print my own colour photographs and make large prints.

I see colour as an amazingly powerful emotional tool. As artists we get to use colour to bring out ambiguous meanings to the images we make and find.

Cinematic is one word that works to describe my images. But it's that tension of nothing happening, and the implication that something is around the corner, that might hook you in.

I have sometimes described my sequences as paper movies. After doing this for 25 years, it never ceases to amaze me what occurs when you combine a picture of a person and a place. When one starts to get a bit more sophisticated with combining images, that's when the analogy of a paper movie starts to evolve.

I always say that the meaning of a photograph resides in the viewer. I found as an adult that Ohio was full of places to make empty pictures, but I do that from a very full disposition.

Picasso once said that "art is a lie that makes us realise the truth". Photography's inherent contradiction is that it is capable of absolutely capturing something real, and at the same time, with a fraction of a second before or after, it also carries the same power to lie. I like to employ this and fluctuate amongst the two while I am working.

In an effort to try and catch or represent some kind of reality, photography shows you how much of a moving target our actuality truly is. I tend to believe that we all create the world that we live in.

With Trump as president, I feel great uncertainty. It's sad to see the erosion of all the positive things we've been moving forward with, not just in [the US] but also around the world.

My new book, *Bright Black World*, contains predominately landscape photos. It's different from my past work as it does not have any relationship with my own personal history, nor is it set in the suburban context. I have in fact been traveling all over the world to photograph the darkness that I see coming, which is very much inspired by Norse mythology and the concept of Fimbulwinter – the endless apocalyptic storm.

We spend our lives searching for home. After spending most of my career looking for that familiarity, which calls out to me to take a photograph, I know this is true for me. This is also reaffirmed through my audience. The best comment I ever received was, "Todd Hido's photographs do something to me, like he remembers my memories, except he has not met me, and I have not met him".

I am happiest exactly where I am at right now. At my home with my almost-grown children, who are doing things that interest them, and with my lady, Marina, painting in her studio. And with my studio staff, hard at work accomplishing things.

toddhido.com

Artful Dodgers Imaging: The go-to photo lab for professional photographers. Specialists in film processing, scanning, and large-format analogue and digital printing.

From the series
Youth Without Age and Life Without Death.
Image © Laura Pannack
laurapannack.com

This month's portrait-based projects focus on identity and locale, from the transgender community in Peru to a lone weather-watcher in Iceland. Interviews by Charlotte Jansen, Alice Zoo and Cat Lachowskyj

The paradox of otherness is at the core of Maria Sturm's *You don't look Native to me*. Her subjects belong to the Lumbee Tribe of North Carolina, the largest tribe in the region with around 55,000 members, with their name taken from the Lumber River of Robeson County. Starting in 2011, Romanian-born, Germany-raised Sturm spent time in Pembroke, the economic, cultural and political centre of the tribe, photographing their daily lives. It opened up questions about visibility, identity and stereotype in the US, where Native Americans are romanticised yet often dismissed. Many tribes remain officially unrecognised, though the sense of identity within the communities is very strong.

On her first visit, Sturm was struck by two aspects: "One was that almost everyone I talked to introduced themselves with their names and their tribe. The other was the omnipresence of Native American symbolism: on street signs, pictures on walls, on cars, on shirts and as tattoos." She attended powwows (where leaders pray to Jesus, another surprise to Sturm) and spent time with locals.

The resulting photographs, often with motifs of smoke and mirrors, literal and metaphorical, represent the binary nature of identity: the way we see ourselves, and the way our image is presented back to us. "I was thinking, 'Why can a Native American not be blond and blue-eyed? Why am I thinking that?'"

Sturm says. "I was striving to create images that challenge our perception and create moments of contradiction that stimulate the viewer's mind to be aware of the ways in which our perception is working."

As always in the US, issues around race and identity are complex and nuanced; culture is intertwined with politics and histories that have been repressed. Questioning her own understanding of what it means to be Native American, analysing her position as an outsider, Sturm hopes to open the topic to those who might foster similar prejudices.

"There are many works exploring Native America and First Nations, from Thomas Easterly's portrait of Keokuk in 1847 to contemporary works such as Kalpesh Lathigra's *Lost in the Wilderness*," Sturm points out. Works like these have defined and identified Native American culture to outsiders for over a century, but few have attempted to dismantle that gaze.

Sturm's project captures Native American identity not as fixed, but as it evolves and redefines itself with the next generation. A key image for her is a portrait of a girl called Kearsey in traditional dress wearing plastic fangs for Halloween. "I was curious to see the community trying on identities for a holiday like Halloween," she says. "I like that picture because she is challenging the viewer with her gaze, she looks fierce and confident, which stands for a new attitude, a new stance." **BJP**

mariasturm.com

Projects

Maria Sturm

When Daragh Soden first visited Toulon in southern France on commission to make a portrait of the city, he wasn't sure what shape the work would take. "It didn't seem like an extraordinary place," he recalls, having accepted an invitation by Studio Be-Pôles to do the next edition of its *Portraits de Villes*, a series of travel notebooks in which artists are given carte blanche to illustrate different cities.

The commission came on the back of winning the Grand Prix at Hyères Festival 2017 for work he'd made about his native Dublin (a picture from which won the Undergraduate Single Image in *BJP*'s Breakthrough Awards in 2016). But Toulon represented a departure for the 28-year-old Irishman, now based in London. He found himself in an unfamiliar environment, and was initially uncertain if he'd be able to bring any depth to the assignment: "There were definitely pictures to be made, but I didn't know what I wanted to say."

Then he began delving into the city's past and connecting its history to its complex present. A port of strategic importance since the days of King Charles VIII, and the departure point for colonisers and adventurers throughout the 18th and 19th centuries, it remains the Mediterranean's biggest naval harbour, and is home to both a large North African community and a sizeable support base for extreme rightwing politics. "I was walking around Toulon with its history in mind," says Soden, noting how often he saw France's national motto adorning the city's impressive Haussmann-designed buildings, connecting the words Liberté, Egalité, Fraternité and their author, Maximilien Robespierre, one of the key figures of the French Revolution, with the contemporary reality of Toulon today.

Searching for the genesis of these ideas, he began reading about how Plato, the father of Western political philosophy, considered society's mythological beliefs and economic inequalities to intersect. "Plato believed that myths used to justify inequalities of wealth and power were essential to preserve order and stability in society," explains the photographer. This belief would be at odds with the French principle of 'Egalité'; and, indeed, despite this supposed cornerstone of post-Revolution French society, Toulon is renowned as a home of the Front National party and their divisive politics. "I wanted to frame the present as a myth, to show that perhaps things aren't so different today, to question the complexities of history… You can have the banner, but then what's the reality?"

The resulting project (launched in book form at The Library Project in Dublin, and exhibited at this year's Hyères festival, just 13 miles from Toulon) is arrestingly dynamic; Soden has a keen eye for human interaction, for atmospheric light and for the narrative that pulses beneath the surface of a place. Throughout the work, for instance, there is a striking contrast between candid beach scenes and the more formalised portraits of military men that Soden made when he spent the day on board a navy boat. Soden used this distinction to play on Plato's myths, and the difference between the society's strata.

"It's these kinds of things that I wanted to touch upon, but not to tell people, not to be too didactic," says Soden. "I think with all of my work, the first thing is to engage people. But I also think it's really important to have work that has layers, work that you can go back to." **BJP**

daraghsoden.com
portraitsdevilles.fr

Daragh Soden

Finding an ethical framework for documenting others while simultaneously bringing exposure to marginalised communities has always been a contentious topic within the medium of photography. For Juan Jose Barboza-Gubo and Andrew Mroczek, this balance is tackled through their relentless repartee, a constant engagement between two friends that leaves no topic or problematic issue unaddressed.

The artist duo met two years ago when Mroczek curated an exhibition of Barboza-Gubo's work, and their persistent conversations resulted in a number of collaborative works on under-represented communities in Barboza-Gubo's hometown of Lima, Peru, including their series, *Virgines de la Puerta*. The project focuses on transgender women living in the city – a community that has been denied basic human rights for centuries and which faces constant threats of hate crimes and violence. "It is the most attacked community in my country," explains Barboza-Gubo. "Denying your masculinity in such a machismo culture is viewed as the worst possible offence, and then you add social class and racism on top of that... It's endless."

In order to create a series that properly represented their subjects, the duo looked extensively at past portrayals of Lima's transgender community. They noticed a visual narrative that focused predominantly on the women's bodies and low-income surroundings. "Sure, these artists are saying something about the community," says Barboza-Gubo. "But I'm not sure they are actually trying to help. In the photo world in particular, there's an importance placed on documenting life in general. But at the same time, it's too lazy to just go and photograph these women in such a voyeuristic way; it's disrespectful. We wanted to show people a different vision of these women that best represents who they are as people."

The resulting images reinstate the women into the cultural Peruvian landscape that systemically rejects them. Collaborating with their subjects, they envision them as important cultural symbols, saints and religious icons, allowing them to show as much or as little of their bodies as they see fit. Soft, warm lighting and lavish surroundings subvert the harsh photojournalism that we are used to associating with these subjects. Instead, they are dressed in traditional regalia crafted by local artisans, forming an osmosis between their bodies and the society that has denied their existence as people.

Ultimately, the duo's intended audience is the women they collaborate with. "The idea that this work is being shown all over the world is a by-product as far as we are concerned. At the heart of this work, our goal is to show these women that they are a legitimate part of their culture." **BJP**

barbozagubo-mroczek.com

Juan Jose Barboza-Gubo
& Andrew Mroczek

"After finishing my studies in photography, I felt as if I had lost all my inspiration. As soon as I landed in Iceland, it all came back, with every step I made." Marzena Skubatz's ongoing project, *The Weather Report*, was born of a desire to escape. Having grown up on a farm, she craved a return to nature, and was seeking a new farm to stay and work on. A chance encounter led her to Marsibil E, a woman who lives and works at the end of a remote fjord in Iceland, reporting on the weather.

Skubatz stayed with Marsibil for eight months before she began to work on the project, just as it was time for her to leave. "I took one picture of her on the last day," she explains. A few months later she returned, and the project began in earnest. It took a long time to build enough of a mutual rapport due to her subject's intense shyness, but during this second trip – with Marsibil E newly alone, her husband having passed away in the interim – she agreed that Skubatz could tell her story.

The project documents the breathtaking sweep of Icelandic winter: gargantuan snow drifts, heavy mist, darkness, steam; as well as Marsibil's smallness in the landscape, checking temperature gauges in a red dressing gown, or illuminated by a fire. Skubatz shadowed her daily work routine, at one stage even accompanying her on the obligatory task of getting up every three hours, curious to see what effect it would have on her mood. Both women were subject to the surrounding meteorological forces, and this feeling of submission and deep respect for the environment is palpable throughout. "I love the constantly changing light and weather," says Skubatz. "Even the snow and the dark winters, which absorb everything around you. They force me to pay attention to details."

Beyond making a record of Marsibil E and her work, Skubatz believes in the value of recording this place at the end of the fjord for posterity, as climate change accelerates its disappearance. Marsibil herself has been witness to these changes, having lived on the farm all her life: "She told me that when she was a child, the sea was much further away, and it's coming closer and closer. So this place will disappear, like many places."

Citing influences such as Alec Soth's *Broken Manual* and Roni Horn's Icelandic works, Skubatz's project is deeply invested in a sense of place, of solitude, and of the elemental force of the natural world. **BJP**

marzenaskubatz.com

Marzena Skubatz

THE PORTRAIT ISSUE

With Brexit on the near horizon, we return with Portrait Of Britain, our nationwide book and exhibition putting citizens centre stage. Jono Rotman discusses his portrait project on New Zealand's notorious Mongrel Mob. Agnès Varda partners with JR to create a portrait of France on the fringes. And Richard Billingham returns to his seminal work, Ray's a Laugh, with his first cinema release

BACK HOME

It was almost by accident that Richard Billingham came to fame with his unflinching images of his chaotic family home in the West Midlands. Now he's returned to the scene to make a feature film – "my attempt to provide a backstory for the photographs," he tells Tom Seymour, who visited him on set in January

2

Multiple jigsaws, almost completed, are laid out in the living room. On the sideboard, porcelain creatures jostle for space with family photos – a marriage scene, a smiling elderly couple, kids in the park. Dolls are piled high on a chair in the corner, arranged in a chaotic arc. White masks, like those from the Venice Carnival, are positioned across one wall. The wallpaper is a scene from a seaside town – spinning Ferris wheels, winding rollercoasters, fairground murals – yet the paper itself is pockmarked with holes and stains.

Richard Billingham, who grew up in this environment, describes the room as "carnivalesque". When he lived here, in Cradley Heath in the West Midlands, he did so with his mother Liz and, after she moved out, his father Ray. This jam of decorative stuff was all Liz. She had winding, flowering roots and flowers tattooed across her arms. She wore floral dresses and she smoked until the ashtrays overflowed.

When Billingham was 10 years old, Ray was laid off from a job as a machinist. The family sold their home for two grand – a cash-in-hand job to a local conman – and moved here, to what was quaintly referred to as public housing. Ray, who until this point only drank in the pub, began his life as a committed alcoholic and a full-time hermit. In the early 1990s, when Billingham was a teenager, Liz moved out, leaving him in the care of Ray – or vice versa. Billingham's younger brother Jason was less studious, more wayward than the quiet, introverted future artist. At the age of 11, he was taken into care. Then, two years later, after Billingham had left home, Ray and Liz reconciled and she moved back in. By this time, Liz had gained pets. "About 10 cats," by Billingham's reckoning. "Hamsters, reptiles, a python, two or three dogs."

However, the room described here isn't a relic of that time. It's a set, a stage. From this remarkably impoverished environment, one of the defining photographers of his generation emerged. And now that artist has returned to his childhood, to the roots of his strange and remarkable life, to make *Ray & Liz*, a feature film of such a "lived experience". In the room next door, Billingham is staring into a monitor, directing the action. One room along, the celebrated director of photography, Daniel Landin, known for his work on Jonathan Glazer's *Under the Skin*, is framing a teenage actor playing teenage Richard, and a pubescent boy playing Jason, in the lens of a large digital camera.

The scene filming today seems humdrum, but actually marked a great turning point in the young boys' lives. Young Richard lies in bed, studying a book of graphic pictures. The younger brother is playing with a handful of small plastic insects. A knock comes at the front door and, knowing their father is drunk in bed, the pair argue about who should open it. An older man in a tired, old suit is let into the house, yet Richard carries on reading his book. Eventually the man, a social worker, steps into the bedroom and informs the boy, with a stoic bluntness, that, while Jason would be taken to live elsewhere, Richard was old enough to remain at home and stick it out.

I ask Billingham about the scene, and the memory of that moment in his lived experience, when we meet later in the year in Kentish Town, north London. He's hard at work editing the film and seems distracted. Despite making a film about his childhood, after basing his career on the photographs he took of his childhood, Billingham does not in any way give the impression he wants to talk about his

childhood. "Was it miserable growing up?" he says in answer to an entirely different question. "I get asked that a lot." He pauses and looks away. "I've just been reading a book called *The Girl With No Name*, about a girl who grew up with monkeys in Colombia. She seems to have fond memories of that."

Billingham's distinct way of communicating is not something he reserves for journalists. Justin Salinger, the actor tasked with playing the part of Ray, Billingham's father, says: "When I first met Richard, I found him very economical with his words, and with the way he communicated what he wanted. He didn't talk about a character, or about thoughts, or about motivations, but very directly, abruptly even, in simple terms. He didn't mess about. He'd say, 'My father would do this, my father wouldn't say that, my father would say it like this.'"

The role of Liz will be in-part played by the star of Channel 4 documentary series *Benefits Street*, White Dee, aka Deirdre Kelly ("As soon as I met her, I just thought she looked and sounded exactly like Liz," says Billingham) with Ella Smith also playing his mother at a different era in her life. Smith has her own take on Billingham's methods. "Once I got to meet Richard, I threw millions of questions at him," she says on the phone from Los Angeles after the shoot has wrapped. "I remember using the word 'compassion' really early on. I asked all about where the compassion was for each other, and he sort of giggled, and I realised that was my middle-class London bubble talking. Talking about compassion is a very normal thing for us. But, if you grow up in a tower block, or if you lose a job and have nothing in the fridge for two years, then compassion is the last thing you're thinking about. I think they were more interested in survival."

"Ella and I were constantly baffled by the detached way with which Richard talks about his parents," Salinger admits. "When Ella mentioned the word compassion one day, he said, 'There was no compassion, there was no passion'. So there was no emotion, even sadness, even anger. That's what their lives were, and they just got on with it. And Richard feels there's no point feeling sad about it or sorry for them, or wallowing in the misery that must have been their lives. But I think he accepts that, and he doesn't judge them, and I don't think he's angry with them, and I think it's a brilliant way of approaching it."

If Billingham lacks for words in real life, then his ability to communicate with mise-en-scène remains deeply compelling. In the scene I was witness to, there are maybe two sentences of dialogue, while the scenario unfolds for minutes on end. His directions are exacting. He tells the boy how to play with the reading glasses he holds in his hand, leaving the camera to focus on the detail as it pans across the room. He's specific about the pauses and breaths between the delivery of the words. The book young Richard reads is picked up by the camera.

Portraits of Ray

Later that afternoon, Salinger is shot playing Ray. He sits in a chair, looking out of the window, with a fag in his hand. There's no dialogue. Nothing discernible happens. The camera simply rests on Salinger's Ray as he lives his quiet, hermetic life. Yet again Billingham knows exactly what he wants from the actor. Each movement he must make is specific and non-negotiable.

1   Ella Smith as Liz on the set of *Ray & Liz*.

2   Tony Way stars as the wayward Uncle Lol.

3   Justin Salinger as father Ray.

4   Richard Billingham (left) on the set of his
    directorial debut, alongside acclaimed director
    of photography, Daniel Landin.

    All images © Rob Baker Ashton.

Further viewing

Following its world premiere at Locarno in
August, *Ray & Liz* is showing at film festivals
including Toronto (06 to 16 September),
New York (28 September to 14 October),
with a UK premiere planned for October.
For updates, visit @rayandlizfilm on Instagram.

"It was strange, and at first quite alien, and it could make the atmosphere tense," Salinger says of being directed in such a way. "He would start sentences with things like, 'Ray wouldn't do that, he would sit like this', or 'One drag of the cigarette, hold it like this, flick it there, move to that side, look at the screen'. It was very detailed work, and the first take I remember feeling incredibly tense, and thinking a thousand things in my head even though there was no dialogue. The second time I thought, 'I've got this, I can do this'. Eventually I was able to find freedom in all those very prescriptive directions. As the film progressed, I got more used to the language, to being able to work like that, and I found it very, very rewarding; an exciting way of working."

Smith remembers walking around the local area where the film was to be shot. "I walked past the library and Richard just said, 'I spent my whole childhood in that library'. That helped me understand his experience. He wasn't in the house, he was out reading, teaching himself." At some point, he bought a book for 37 pence about wildlife mammals. He read it again and again before trying his hand at sketching the animals from within its pages. Paper and pencils were one of the few things he could get his hands on. Billingham found in such drawings a way of dealing with the long hours alone in the house with his father. He would be an artist, he decided, and started to apply to art schools. He applied, in writing, to 16 of them and in the post came 16 rejection letters.

At 18, Billingham eventually received an acceptance letter, for an art foundation course at Bournville College of Art in Birmingham. He would stack shelves at a supermarket in the evening and catch the bus every morning, journeying across the Black Country and into the city. For the first time, he gained a focused tutorship in the arts, and turned his attention from drawing to painting. Ray, he decided, would be a convenient figure to paint. "But it was difficult to get him to stay still for more than 15 or 20 minutes," Billingham says. "He'd end up asking for a drink. I thought, 'If I can take a photograph of Ray, I can use it as a basis for my painting.'"

New sensation

Billingham kept his photographs of Ray and Liz hidden for a long time. After Bournville, he enrolled at the University of Sunderland. His photographs were kept in a plastic bag in his student room. The photographer Julian Germain came to the university to give a lecture, and Billingham was struck by how Germain would talk about photographs from a structural perspective. He built up the courage to show Germain the contents of the plastic bag. "Julian would look at them and say, 'That's a fuckin' great photo, that is,'" Billingham says today. "But he wanted to talk to me about the framing and light and composition, and I liked that."

The pair stayed in touch after Billingham graduated. Over the course of a couple of years, as Billingham stacked shelves in Kwik Save, they hatched a plan to publish his first photography book. *Ray's a Laugh* came out in 1996, published by Scalo. Copies were acquired by Charles Saatchi, who would go on to include Billingham's photographs in his exhibition *Sensation*, the infamous 1997 showcasing of many of the so-called Young British Artists of the time at the Royal Academy of Arts in London. Billingham's cheap photographs of Ray and Liz were shown alongside early works by Damien Hirst, Gillian Wearing, Sarah Lucas, Mat Collishaw and Tracey Emin. The exhibition was controversial. It showed Hirst's tiger shark in a formaldehyde tank, Emin's *Everyone I Have Ever Slept With* tent and Marcus Harvey's huge portrait of the 'Moors Murderer' Myra Hindley, made up of prints of children's hands.

Yet Billingham's photography sparked as much debate as anything else in the show. The discussion came from the distinct timbre of the photography. Billingham's work could be seen as classic vérité documentary, but they were also clearly private and personal photographs. They were confessional, relational, deeply connected to his own being, yet at a remove and distant – as if he were set apart from something that also consumed him. For he wasn't just photographing his parents; it was as if Billingham was invisible, oblivious. Ray and Liz seemed entirely unconcerned by the act of being photographed, as if they were totally unaware of what their son was doing. Or they just didn't care.

As his profile rose, with the Deutsche Börse Photography Prize in 1997 and a nomination for the Turner Prize in 2001, critics questioned where he was coming from, what his point was. Was this a tacit or explicit reaction to the government policies of the day? Was it proof that poverty is some sort of moral failing? Was this a politicised, liberal look at the working classes, or poverty porn?

Expect those questions to be rehashed again when *Ray & Liz* is released in a Britain preparing to leave the EU, and still coming to terms with the class gulfs that the referendum exposed. Yet Billingham's answer will remain consistent – that he was just trying to make sense of where he was. He was using the camera as a way to mediate the space between himself and his hermetic, mostly silent father.

"Watching Richard on set, it was like he would create new images of his parents," Salinger says. "He brought a camera onto the set, and you'd find him placing objects in the background and taking pictures. Usually the focus, almost more than the acting, was on the still images, on what was in the frame. That was a completely different way of working from what I'm used to. But it was fascinating to be around."

Strikingly, Billingham recalls moments in his youth when his life felt like that of a constructed drama. "The film is my attempt to provide a backstory for the photographs," he says. "When I was still living with Ray, I thought of the situation as a film. The film was already taking place in my head at that point."

"The film is a reflective process, for Richard is now able to look at his childhood from a distance," says the film's producer, Jacqui Davies. "He's not trying to contextualise it politically or socially, to say it was good or bad. It's a way of showing how Richard experienced life at that time – so it's very slow, all in one space."

"He doesn't function like any other director I've ever worked with," says Smith. "But it's very refreshing, because he's fastidious about his truth. He's honouring it in a way that feels right for him – because he lived it. When he creates something that feels authentic to him, you could see his face light up. I don't know if it's cathartic, but I'm sure it affected him."

The film is a triptych, exploring three separate chapters of Billingham's early life with Ray, Liz and Jason. The first chapter, dated around 1980, centres on the time Jason was put in the care of Uncle Lol for an afternoon. Lol gets blind drunk, and Jason goes missing. In the second chapter, we meet Jason as a misbehaving pubescent teen whose misdemeanours include tipping chilli powder into Ray's mouth while he sleeps. Yet to focus on the plot would miss the true meaning of the film. Filmmakers often talk about personal projects, films made out of passion. Few have gone to the lengths that Billingham has to create something that meant so much – in a purely internal way.

"We would be shooting a scene, and Richard would suddenly focus on a corner of the room that wouldn't necessarily even be in shot," Smith says. "And he would stop and say, 'That mark on the wall shouldn't be there, it should be here.' That goes to show the level he would fixate on such things. At first, if it wasn't right he would obviously feel uncomfortable. He had to learn to deal with it, and to make compromises along the way, which he did with real charm."

It's a dog's life

Billingham has a very different life now. After the shoot, he will return home to Swansea, where he lives with his long-term partner, three small children and unruly, boisterous dogs. He's a visiting professor in art at the University of Gloucestershire and Middlesex University, and his new family is the subject of his more recent photography. One photograph shows a spacious, beautifully furnished living room framing a smiling toddler staring at a whippet. In another, two children play on a trampoline and slide in a waterlogged garden. He has spent time focusing on the landscapes near his family home – they're bucolic and pastoral, the work of someone who seems very happy to be where he is. They're nice pictures, and they work in comparison to those of his childhood with Ray and Liz, but, taken on their own terms, they're frictionless, uncomplicated photographs. It's fair to say Billingham has never found another subject that touched a nerve like Ray and Liz.

The fact this film is being made serves as an acknowledgement of how much Billingham's early years impacted on his later life. So is this therapy for him? "I don't think he is dong it for catharsis, personally," says Smith. "I can't speak for him, but my instinct says he's just doing this right now, and then he'll do something else. He's not someone who has deep angst in him, as far as I can tell. He's not someone who has deep pain. The more you ask about his life, the more he giggles about it. If he does have any hurt about it, he's not a haunted person, he's a joyful person. And that's what is really hard, because a lot of people get into this industry because they're trying to have this catharsis. I'm sure most of us are, but he's different." **BJP**

ON THE ROAD

*Agnès Varda teams up with artist JR for an Oscar-nominated film, reflecting on the role of chance in her work as one of France's most influential filmmakers, and journeying together across their homeland to create a portrait of its people.
Words by Tom Seymour*

Previous page: Agnès Varda and JR walking in front of a slag heap in Liévin, northern France, while making *Faces Places*.

Above: Varda and JR pose with a collage of the workers at the Arkema factory in Château-Arnoux-Saint-Auban.

Right: The inhabitants of Pirou, Normany, in front of their pictures on the side of an abandoned building in the village.

"Chance has always been my best asset," Agnès Varda says of creating *Faces Places*, her latest film, made on the eve of her 90th birthday, and co-directed with the French street artist JR, known for his huge open-air photographic exhibitions. "As always in documentaries – and I've done lots of them – you have an idea. But before long, chance enters into play, and suddenly things congeal to focus on a specific person or place."

Faces Places 'congeals' in remarkable ways, reflecting on a pivotal era in the French hinterlands, the role imagery plays in our collective lives, and the likely final journey of photographer-turned-filmmaker Agnès Varda, one of the greatest artists of her time. The film is a road trip, in time-honoured cinematic fashion, between two artists who have spent their lives exploring how images can be created, displayed and shared. To be released in British cinemas on 21 September, the film has earned Varda an Oscar nomination for Best Documentary Feature, making her the oldest nominee of an Academy Award ever.

The lives of Varda and JR are worlds apart, and there is an age gap of 55 years between the pair. She was introduced to the 35-year-old photographer through her daughter, Rosalie, before he visited her in her home and studio on Rue Daguerre in Montparnasse, Paris. There, they devised a plan: to drive through France, visiting its towns and villages and meeting people along the way, as she has done in her films and documentaries – from *Cléo From 5 to 7* and *Le Bonheur*, made in the 1960s, to *Vagabond* from 1985 and *The Gleaners and I* in 2000 – throughout her life.

They took off in JR's van, which he has converted into a mobile studio to create his trademark gargantuan artworks, reproducing his street portraits as multi-sheet posters pasted onto the side of buildings. Together, the pair invited whoever they found to pose, before pasting,

in head-spinning scale, the resulting portraits onto the places their subjects call home. Varda is delighted with the idea, even if, on the surface, it seems rather more modest than many of the films she has made throughout her career. As the film wears on, we start to guess at why. We realise her ability to recall her life is starting to fail her. Her eyesight is fading quickly too, and the film pauses so we can watch her undergo queasy eye surgery. Finally, as her 10th decade approaches, her mobility is starting to fail her. She's compelled to "photograph faces so they don't fall into the hole of memory".

She has started, she admits in the film, to consider her own death. "Every new person I meet feels like my last one," she says. This mournful feeling calcifies as they pay their respects in the cemetery where Henri Cartier-Bresson is buried and, somewhat disastrously, try and pay a visit to an old friend, now a reclusive and bitter old man called Jean-Luc Godard. Varda has spent much of her life referred to as an afterthought of the very male nouvelle vague, the aesthetic and politically revolutionary movement in French cinema that arrived in the decades after the denouement of the Second World War, and centred around the creative works of figures such as Godard, François Truffaut, Claude Chabrol, Jacques Rivette, Éric Rohmer and her late husband, Jacques Demy. But in many respects she was a forerunner – and photography played a key role.

The beginning of Varda's career in film is often identified as *La Pointe Courte*, her debut feature, made when she was barely 27 years old. It came out in 1955, a full five years before Godard released *Breathless*, and was widely credited with launching the nouvelle vague. Yet few realise Varda was primarily a photographer before, during and after its making. In a 2015 interview with *Sight & Sound*, she said: "I took photographs of everything I wanted to film. The photographs are almost models for the shots. And I started making films with the sole experience of photography – that is to say, [asking] where to place the camera, at what distance, with which lens and what lights?"

La Pointe Courte follows the stylised conversations of a married couple sensing their end, located as much from the female perspective as the male. Yet the film is notable, on modern viewing, for another very Varda-esque quality: unlike the works of many of her nouvelle vague contemporaries, *La Pointe Courte* shows a willingness to explore, without judgement or sentimentality, the ground-level lives of France's rural poor. Her interest in fellow French folk who lived lives far from the bohemian affluence of Paris was apparent in her first film, and is equally apparent in what will likely be her last. Varda "loves the country", she says. "We quickly hit on the idea of villages. That's where we'd meet people, and that's what happened." Yet *Faces Places* was made in a very key moment for France. Varda sees the film as "a modest project in a period of widespread chaos".

Varda is a true creation of the Rive Gauche, a woman with family money behind her, and the means to allow her to spend much of her youth exploring her education. She was born in 1928 to a large middle-class family then based in Belgium, and during the Second World War they lived on a boat in Sète, the Mediterranean port on France's southern coast famous for its artistic heritage. Varda was 17 when the war ended. The family moved to Paris, where she attended the Lycée Victor-Duroy, a prestigious school in the 7th arrondissement, before studying for a degree in literature and psychology at the Sorbonne, and then on to an art history degree at the École du Louvre, and finally a formal education in photography at the Vaugirard school of photography and the École des Beaux-Arts. Given her background, and the life she's led, it's fair to guess that Varda is not a big fan of Marine

Le Pen, nor is she sympathetic to the virulent far-right nationalism that made her the second most voted-for politician in France. *Faces Places* was shot in the run-up to the 2017 French elections, with large tracts of rural and ageing France placing their faith in the openly racist and divisive vision of Le Pen's Front National party. Varda and JR, therefore, spent their time in many of the villages and towns that would have voted in large numbers for Le Pen. They visit the coal-mining regions of northern France, now pockmarked with abandoned and dilapidated homes. The sky is overcast, and the humble terraces are built with red brick. This is France's version of the Rust Belt, or the post-industrial towns and villages you find across Yorkshire, Durham and Wales. They speak to former miners, waitresses, factory workers and dockworkers – not, if the current liberal worldview is to be believed, the kind of people who would be hugely welcoming of two Parisian artists turning up in their village with a bunch of cameras and a point to make.

But, in testament to Varda and JR's simple, unwavering belief in the power of the image, the people they meet and photograph along the way open themselves up in the most moving of ways. Politics is never mentioned. The film, instead, is about the people they met representing themselves as they pleased. They hear stories from Jeannine, the last inhabitant in a row of miners' homes that are scheduled for destruction, who cries when her portrait is pasted to the side of her precarious home. "She talked about her father who was a miner, and the former miners shared some beautiful stories about a world we know little about," says Varda. "It was interesting to hear them talk with such fervour. We were touched by Jeannine." They meet a farmer who, in solitary isolation, works thousands of acres of land, and paste his portrait on the side of his barn. They meet a trio of dockworkers from Le Havre, in the midst of a strike over working conditions –

although, at Varda's insistence, their wives' views are involved too. One of the dockworkers says to the filmmakers: "Art is for everyone, no?" after witnessing colleagues pasted onto the factory walls. "Art is for everyone," Varda reiterates. "The dockworkers agreed to help us because they were keen to participate in an artistic project."

It's experiences like this, Varda says, that have always drawn her to the documentary form. "You spend a few days with people, you become friends, then you lose touch with them, just like the way you depict them with large ephemeral images that will vanish from the walls. These moments are magical. The moment of meeting people, the moment of filming, pasting, and voilà…"

In his review in IndieWire, David Ehrlich writes: "Varda and JR aren't validating their subjects, but rather asking them to help corroborate the idea that images are a way of affirming our existence, of being bigger than our bodies." Varda has become bigger than her body of work. The film is a tribute to an artist who, while she has to strain to see the work she has created, and while she can't climb a set of stairs in order to see a huge mural from a vantage point, or walk without using a cane, can still demonstrate an intuitive ability to bring her subjects out of themselves, to become more of themselves for her camera.

The feeling that this may be Varda's final film – indeed, her final journey around France – is never mentioned. That, long after the other names of the nouvelle vague have disappeared from public view, she will now quietly slip into retirement too. Towards the film's end, JR takes Varda to a moody, deserted beach in Normandy, near a village call Saint-Aubin-sur-Mer, a spot where he often goes to ride motorcycles. He takes her to a huge German military bunker left over from the war, which has since fallen off the decaying cliff. It now resides in the middle of the beach, where it came to rest,

sticking up on one end. Varda is filmed seemingly unaware of where they're heading. Then, as they drive through the village and onto the beach, she suddenly recognises it, a distant memory suddenly taking form. "Wait, I know Saint-Aubin-sur-Mer," she says. "I came here with Guy Bourdin." Varda had travelled here with the now iconic fashion photographer in the 1950s, when he was beginning to work for *Vogue Paris*. Varda takes JR to Bourdin's former house nearby. "Remembering the dead is good," she says. "He went on to become a famous photographer, but when I knew him, he was a young fellow from La Chapelle-sur-Dun who lived with his grandmother." Although they never worked with each other professionally, Bourdin would often pose for Varda. "He was a good model, because he understood what I wanted to do," she says.

She reveals the small, aged photographs she took of him back in the 1950s. One shows a young man, stripped bare, sat on the wall of a crumbling house. Another, naked, in a pool of light within a cavernous ruin. Another shows him relaxing on the beach, his legs stretched out. "Feels like it was yesterday," she says. "I may remember the photos of him better than I remember him." "Why don't we put that image on the bunker?" JR asks. The pasting of Bourdin onto the bunker shows how skilled JR and his team are. They were working against the tide and a fierce wind, their ladders bouncing against the concrete. Yet, against such conditions, JR had the foresight to tilt the portrait of Bourdin so his body follows the shape of the bunker. Bourdin looked "like a child in his cradle," Varda says, "resting in peace".

When they return the next morning, the photo has been washed away. "I was moved by how the meaning of the photo was transformed, of what it briefly became," Varda says. "Then in came the tide and washed it away. The photograph vanished, and we will vanish too." **BJP**

Left: Jeannine in the doorway of her home – the last inhabited house in a row of miners' cottages – adorned with her portrait, in Bruay-la-Buissière, northern France.

Above: Portrait of Guy Bourdin, photographed by Agnès Varda in 1954, on the side of an old Second World War bunker on the beach at Saint-Aubin-sur-Mer.

All images © Agnès Varda-JR-Ciné-Tamaris/Social Animals 2016.

Further viewing

Faces Places is released in British cinemas on 21 September. A retrospective of eight of Varda's best-known films is available online at Curzon Home Cinema.
curzonartificialeye.com/faces-places
curzonhomecinema.com/collections/agnes_varda_collection

PORTRAIT OF BRITAIN

As Brexit negotiations reach their denouement, we return with the country's biggest public art exhibition. Putting the British people centre stage on JCDecaux screens across the land, and commemorating their unique diversity and traditions in a new collaboration with Hoxton Mini Press, we give pause to reflect on who we are – a nation of individuals

3

4

11

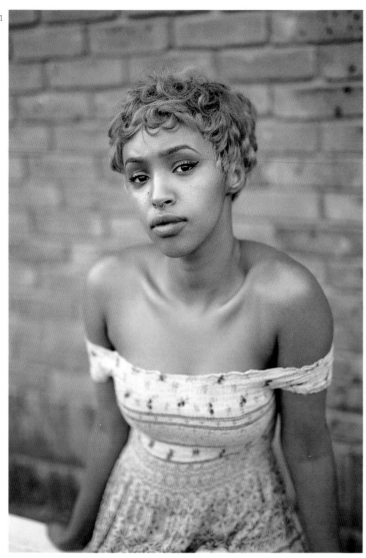

13

12

14

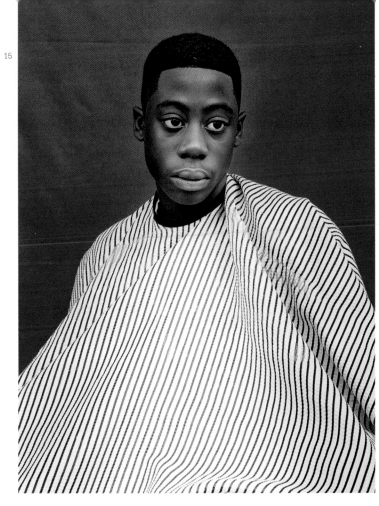

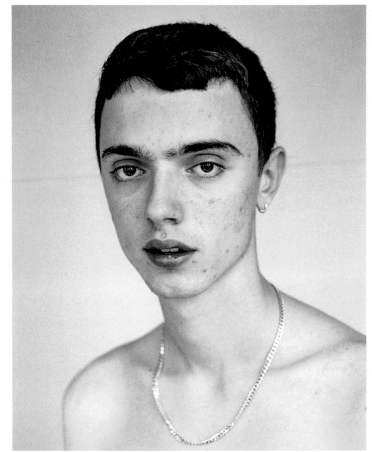

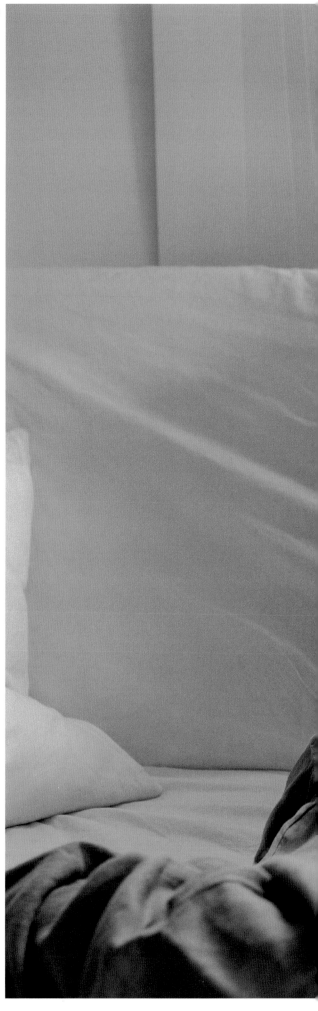

Further viewing

26

The 100 winners from Portrait Of Britain 2018
can be seen on selected JCDecaux screens across
the UK throughout September.
The book, published by Hoxton Mini Press, priced
£20, features the full shortlist of 200 portraits,
together with information about the subjects
and quotes from the photographers, and an
introduction by Will Self.
portraitofbritain.uk
hoxtonminipress.com
jcdecaux.co.uk

1   *Simon* © Eliška Kyselková.

2   *British Soldier* © Jorge Gutierrez.

3   *The Flash* © Alex Ingram.

4   *DCI Andy Shearwood* © Rory Mulvey.

5   *Samuel Froggatt* © Craig Waddell.

6   *Capreese, 18 years old* © Michelle Sank.

7   *Linda* © Matt Grayson.

8   *Untitled* © Polly Alderton.

9   *Dave* © Dan Wood.

10 *Kerena at St Kathrines Hill*
    © Kim Jakobsen To.

11 *Balqis* © Anselm Ebulue.

12 *Joseph* © Leticia Valverdes.

13 *Isaac Dapo Chukwumah*
    © Arabelle Zhuang.

14 *Olivia* © Aurelia Chiffe.

15 *Tumise* © Christoph Soeder.

16 *Isaac* © Matt Grayson.

17 *Louis* © James Greenhalgh.

18 *Felicia* © John Davis.

19 *Luka* © Alvaro Lopez Gimenez.

20 *Temple*, *Job*, *Truth and Pierre*
    © Maja Daniels.

21 *Joe and Duke* © Peter Zelewski.

22 *Noon Flowers* © Anaïs Zamboni.

23 *Mr and Mrs MacDonald* © Craig Easton.

24 *Chi and Marloe* © Iringó Demeter.

25 *Eric* © Simon Martin.

26 *Mao* © Steven Barritt.

27 *Nala* © Julia Fullerton-Batten.

28 *Tyburn Convent* © Doma Dovgialo.

29 *Mod & Rocker* © Emma Martin.

"These magnificent photographs capture at once the great diversity and the inescapable identity of the British," writes Will Self in the introduction to a new book featuring the 200 shortlisted images from this year's Portrait Of Britain. "Gay, straight, bisexual and non-normative; male, female and non-binary; old, young and in between – how can it be that these – every one a compelling identity in its own right – are nonetheless trumped by a Britishness as heavy and irresistible as a Dundee fruit cake?"

Identity is a complex enough question for us as individuals, but talk about a country – in this case, one going through some serious soul-searching – and then the question becomes more loaded. The 200 photographs in this year's Portrait Of Britain don't provide any easy answers. But in a period during which we are constantly fed the narrative of a country divided, they provide a timely reminder that a nation is made up of individuals, not just the sum of our tribal affiliations. Each portrait is a story in itself. And collectively they present an alternative to the political rhetoric, a human face that gives some nuance to the picture of who we are.

Visualised as an exhibition by the people, of the people and for the people, Portrait Of Britain was initiated as an open call for images that celebrate the country's unique heritage and diversity. The result is public art on a huge scale – a countrywide exhibition that puts the nation's citizens centre stage in bustling public spaces. Thanks to our partnership with JCDecaux, with its huge network of digital screens up and down the land, 100 of the portraits will take over high streets, shopping centres, airports and railway stations once again throughout September, confronting the public with a reflection of themselves as they go about their daily business. Taken from all walks of life, these subjects share the same space, from humble bus depots to great shopping cathedrals. With each image appearing on screens for five to 10 seconds, the effect is a lingering glance, witnessed by millions of passers-by.

This year we have also collaborated with one of our favourite publishers, Hoxton Mini Press, to display all 200 shortlisted photographs. Presented as a 336-page hardback book, designed by Shaz Madani, it offers the chance to be a bit more nosy, to see the pictures all together – a record of an important era, and the opportunity to consider not just who we are, but where we come from and where we are going. BJP

CHAPTER AND VERSE

*Both fascinating and unnerving,
Jono Rotman's portraits of notorious
New Zealand gang members, the Mongrel
Mob, challenge perceptions of a group
feared by mainstream society.
Words by Allie Haeusslein*

Arresting. Exquisite. Gripping. Chilling. Disgraceful. Unacceptable. These are all words people have used to describe portraits made by Jono Rotman. Created over the last decade, his project *Mongrelism* presents an intimate look at members of the Mongrel Mob – New Zealand's largest, most notorious gang. Though he is looking at a subculture as an outsider – a domain regularly mined by photojournalists – Rotman eschews a traditional documentarian approach to his subject matter. In so doing, the project's scope extends beyond the Mob itself to touch upon issues related to New Zealand's charged colonial past and self-professed biculturalism, the politics and ethics of portraiture, and the intersections of seemingly disparate human experience.

The New Zealand-born photographer explains that since childhood, "I always felt certain violent and uneasy forces within my country". In *Lockups* (1999-2005), Rotman photographed the interiors of prisons and psychiatric hospitals throughout New Zealand, exploring the medium's ability to convey the fraught "psychic climate" embedded in these state-controlled institutions. The works are eerily devoid of people, a deliberate decision made, says Rotman, "because I wanted to encourage a direct, personal interaction with the spaces. With prisons, for example, as soon as you introduce people into the picture, it becomes easy to think, 'Here's the storyline: this place is for those sorts of people. And I can fit it all into my established worldview'". By removing such easily construed markers, Rotman forces the viewer to engage closely with the details that are present, considering what those visual cues convey about what it feels like to be incarcerated and, perhaps also about New Zealand past and present, and the nature of culturally ingrained predispositions.

Following *Lockups*, Rotman was "thinking about male power and the extremes of how that is presented in the human experience". He remembers, "On the one side, you have established modes of corporate, military and state control. For me, 'gangism' is on the same spectrum of group adherence. Only with gangs, it's committing to something beyond the established social ecology." Through contacts suggested by a gang liaison within the police force, Rotman initially planned to photograph members of various New Zealand gangs, estimates of which indicate there are 25 affiliations on the small islands nation, with a total membership that outnumbers the country's own army. "It is a fertile subject," he explains. "But for me, the Mongrel Mob ultimately felt like they have the most unique identity, the most searing percolation of the forces at play."

Since emerging in the early 1960s, the Mongrel Mob has grown to more than 30 chapters with a carefully developed and fostered reputation produced through committing some of the country's most notorious crimes. Early members describe the group's inception as a response to the poor treatment and abuse they endured while in state care. Although the founding members were primarily white, the majority of today's Mob members are Maori, a group that has, despite proclamations of shared sovereignty since the 19th century, suffered continued marginalisation and subjugation. The inequity and discrimination experienced by many of the gang's Maori members has also fuelled the Mob's evolution.

Mongrel Mob members typically wear red and black, and are identified by their elaborately tattooed faces. These tattoos usually feature a combination of the gang's name, its symbol – an English bulldog, sometimes donning a Second World War-style German helmet – and the swastika. This loaded iconography emblazoned across their faces reflects both an aggressive response to their feeling of long-standing mistreatment (by the government of young men in state care, and by British colonisers of indigenous Maori) and the gang's commitment to offending mainstream society through a generalised 'fuck you' ethos.

Though this charged backstory provides an intrinsically fascinating human-interest narrative, *Mongrelism* resists this reading in favour of something with greater nuance and wider relevance. From the start, Rotman aspires to refrain from a subjective exploration and interpretation of the Mongrel Mob in favour of "transmitting their spirit while still letting them retain their mystery and privacy". He made the first portraits in a formal studio space with strobe lighting. The results, however, troubled him both aesthetically and morally. "Using strobes anaesthetised their breath and the portraits seemed to lack a certain soul," he recalls. "Also there was a whole lot of tricky cultural precedent that began to dawn on me. In the studio, it felt like there was an incorrect power dynamic." He opted instead to go to them, shooting the men in front of a plain backdrop at their homes using only the available natural light. Rotman's decision not only created a more challenging environment for shooting, but also altered the experience of the shoot for his sitters.

"Because I'm shooting large format with natural light, the process is really slow," he explains. "So I have to give them a preamble: 'You're going to sit. Then I'm going to focus and mess around with the camera, and you can't move.' It creates a ceremonial process which, in effect, takes us both out of our roles." The resulting portraits attest to a relationship of mutual understanding.

The unprecedented trust and access given to Rotman by this secretive group is echoed in his sense of responsibility to his subjects and their communities, a notable deviation from troubling examples of exploiting people seen as 'other' throughout photography's history. "Because of their trust and what was being gifted to me in their engagement, I have a responsibility to them that the work is not something that I just take away from them. The project's relationship to them is really important to both the spirit and power of the work."

Rotman and Mob members jointly developed a protocol based on transparency and sharing; he shows them work in progress and discusses how he plans to carry it out into the world. While it has not always been easy to stand steadfast when his artistic integrity is in potential jeopardy, Rotman firmly defends the intimate involvement of the Mob in the project's evolution. The work is far stronger, he explains, because "it carries the weight of their presence within it".

Rotman's portraits do not indiscriminately corroborate the mainstream dialogue about the Mob, but rather complicate widely held views. "The idea was that they would be arresting images because of the iconography and aesthetic qualities of the gang, but once you've been drawn in by that, you'd be forced to contend with the weight of human experience and whether the experiences of those men can be read into the topography of their faces." His completed portraits, presented as detailed, larger-than-life-sized colour prints, do just that. An uncomfortable tension between aversion and seduction elicits a visceral confrontation with the work. The immediacy of their conspicuous and, at times, fearsome appearances disconcerts the viewer. We see unnerving tattoos, disquieting expressions, patch-laden clothing, and other gang-related insignia. And we can surmise that these are men who have supported and/or committed terrible crimes, and likely had them visited upon themselves. The question is why? Why have these men, for several generations now, continued to turn to this particular manifestation of community? Why is mainstream integration untenable to them?

Like the vacant spaces in *Lockups*, these photographs are void of context beyond the lone subject, leaving the viewer to grapple with the available information and details. They recall Richard Avedon's *In the American West*, where his outsiders were positioned in front of blank backgrounds so that, in the words of Max Kozloff, "Nothing competes with the presentation of their poor threads, nothing of the personal environment, nothing that might situate, inform and support

Page 69   Bung-Eye Notorious, Te Poho
           O Rāwiri.

Page 70   Shano Rogue, Raukokore.

Page 72   Greco Notorious South Island,
           Tapairu.

Page 73   Taranaki, Purepo.

Page 74   Toots King Country, Te Kūiti.

Page 75   Triple J Notorious' Smokey, Waipawa.

Page 76   Denimz' Patch 49, Porirua.

Page 77   Denimz' Patch 47, Porirua.

Page 78   Denimz' Collage 02, Porirua.

           All images from the series *Mongrelism*
           © Jono Rotman.

Further viewing

Mongrelism is showing at Festival
Images Vevey in Switzerland from
08 to 30 September. A book of the work
is published by Here Press.
images.ch
herepress.org

"The idea was that they would be arresting images because of the iconography and aesthetic qualities of the gang, but once you've been drawn in by that, you'd be forced to contend with the weight of human experience and whether the experiences of those men can be read into the topography of their faces"

a person in the real world, or even in a photograph". As we continue to look closely at Rotman's sitters, subtleties start to reveal themselves: age, distinctive facial features, tones of flesh, and the quality of their postures, gestures and eye contact. Though formally deadpan, there is a sensitivity characterising Rotman's depictions of his Mongrel Mob subjects, one that encourages viewers to confront the difficult truth of our shared humanity. And it is this unexpectedly tender view of a nationally vilified group that underscored the polarising reception of the work during its first major exhibition in New Zealand.

In 2014, eight of Rotman's Mongrel Mob portraits were shown at the Gow Langsford Gallery in Auckland. The exhibition provoked heated public debate and media criticism, especially given that one of the included subjects was then on trial for murder with the victim's father pleading to the gallery and artist to remove the photograph. A spokesperson from an anti-crime advocacy group deplored the work, asserting, "I think it is glorifying gang culture and completely offensive to their victims, and the members of the public and society who live a socially acceptable and tolerated life".

What lies at the heart of this argument is who deserves to be photographed and in what way. Should individuals we might otherwise turn away – those living socially 'unacceptable' lives – be excluded from photographs? Rotman intimates, "It's OK to see a black-and-white, documentary photograph of someone from a difficult environment because that representation fits into the way they're codified within the mainstream narrative." His photographs resist the expected; they do not recall police mugshots or *National Geographic*-style, ethnographic studies of faraway tribes. They bear a stronger resemblance to 19th-century portrait paintings. They are dignified portraits impelling viewer introspection about the source of his or her discomfort and confronting the belief that art is bad or amoral because it triggers uneasiness or indignation.

After speaking in person and at length with Rotman, the victim's father understood his unpopular decision to leave the photograph on view: "It's his work of many, many years… He is not a bad man, one of the best I've met," he told television network TVNZ. "He sticks to his values. He doesn't compromise his beliefs. I've learned a lot. Hopefully I'll come out a better man."

While the work has not been shown in depth outside New Zealand, *Mongrelism* will soon reach a greater audience as a book (made possible through support from the Book Award of the Grand Prix Images Vevey 2017/18 and published by Here Press), which will be released during the Festival Images Vevey this autumn. Rotman's edit and sequencing aims to "illustrate the depth and complexity of their world, but, at the same time, give nothing away". Though the portraits remain central, the book introduces landscapes, close-up studies of gang regalia, single vernacular images, collages hung in members' homes, and a lengthy series of transcribed conversations between various members and the photographer. He intentionally excluded wider footage from his travels with the gang, believing that "anything that might be deduced from that material is contained within the DNA of the work I'm including. Each single image is a vessel of their entire ecology". The book solidly affirms that the Mongrel Mob is a family. While the average person may be unable to relate to the content of the Mob's snapshots or their tattered keepsakes, the broader corollary – family albums, inherited heirlooms, a place to call your own – is universal.

While the book is designed as a vehicle for Rotman's work, it has also, importantly, been designed as a handbook for the Mongrel Mob community. Within the book's fabric is an archive of genealogical, hierarchical and geographic information. It also acts as an oral history, serving as a medium for the voices of high-ranking leaders who have since passed away. The book's dual identity speaks to the project as a symbiotic exchange: the work fuels Rotman's artistic vision and simultaneously links back to the community in an impactful way. A tangible metric of Rotman's effect on the Mongrel Mob community is the integration of his photographs into their everyday lives, appearing on the walls of Mob homes intermingled with their own snapshots and even as markers on their gravestones.

A project like *Mongrelism* has the potential to inspire contemplation and, in the best of circumstances, challenges viewers to evaluate the nature of their entrenched values or preconceptions. While some New Zealanders may dismiss the work, Rotman's photographs generate dialogue and engagement, with implications reaching beyond his depicted subject matter. And perhaps more introspective, multifaceted conversations about these seemingly unpleasant issues will give opportunities to turn towards them, with interest and concern, rather than away in apathetic fear and loathing. **BJP**

jonorotman.com

#FEELAUSTRIA

To feel and to experience life, we feed our inner artist.

Tom O. Marsh, musician

 Austria
arrive
and revive

austria.inf

Gustav Mahler's composing cottage, Steinbach am Atterse

Intelligence

This month we talk to NayanTara Gurung Kakshapati, founder of Photo Kathmandu. Plus we meet Emily Keegin of *The Fader*, and Damien Demolder asks whether the claims of photographic excellence made for Huawei's P20 Pro are phoney

On a mission in Kathmandu

Spurred by the momentum of the People's Movement in Nepal, NayanTara Gurung Kakshapati returned home in 2006 with a mission to build bonds and foster new visual narratives about her homeland. Daniel Boetker-Smith talks to her about her quest ahead of the third edition of Photo Kathmandu, the festival she founded.

In 2006, after a decade of civil war between Maoist revolutionaries and forces loyal to the world's last Hindu monarchy, events reached their crescendo in Nepal with the surrender of King Gyanendra and the declaration of a secular republic. Earlier that year, as the People's Movement (known in Nepal as the Jana Andolan) gathered strength, NayanTara Gurung Kakshapati returned home from her studies in the US to participate, agitating for democracy and an end to war and imperial rule.

Twelve years later, the now director of Photo Kathmandu festival, Kakshapati tells me of this tumultuous time. "I had been overseas for a few years, studying politics and art, and on returning home I got swept up in the euphoria of what I call the 'Kathmandu Spring'. I was one of many young photographers documenting that process of transition." Amidst all the upheaval that followed, she established Photo.Circle, a platform for Nepalese photographers to network and learn from each other, figuring out ways to market and publish their work. "There was so much going on politically and socially, it was very complex and messy," says Kakshapati, who'd

come to the realisation that photography could be used as a tool to enact change, not just document events and tell stories. "Photo.Circle was a way to try to address this situation, to create a space to bring together a community of photographers. It was the right time to try to engage, to share, to learn and to grow." They began with monthly get-togethers, where they would present and discuss work, progressing to making workshops, books and exhibitions.

Skip forward more than a decade and the Photo.Circle team is now preparing to present the third edition of Photo Kathmandu, a festival running from 12 October to 16 November in Patan, just across the Bagmati River from the capital, Kathmandu. Kakshapati tells me this year's festival touches on themes around gender, identity and sexuality, set within a local and global context. "Photo.Circle was established at a moment when the economy, and the country more generally, had been ravaged by 10 years of war. Large numbers of people had left the country during that period and we, as a photographic community, were trying to create a forum for marginalised groups to come together. The festival was established with the Nepali public in mind; we have always catered to that audience by showing photography in work and community spaces. We ensure that we publish in the mainstream media here in Kathmandu to engage all strata of the community, and we organise a significant amount of free public events and programming."

This year's event features a number of workshops, residencies and exhibitions, among them Laurence Rasti's poetic and powerful *There are No Homosexuals in Iran*,

and Sohrab Hura's *The Lost Head and the Bird* [2]. Importantly, both artists are visiting the festival in October to engage with the local community. "We have a long-standing working relationship with Sohrab; he has taught many workshops and mentored many young Nepali photographers both formally and informally. We are excited to show his work for the first time here, and to allow Sohrab the mentor to become Sohrab the artist. His new work is quite experimental and unexpected, and we are really excited to expose young Nepali practitioners to different ways of working and pushing boundaries. Laurence Rasti's work fits seamlessly with our themes of identity, sexuality and gender this year. I met her at Fotomuseum Winterthur Museum in Switzerland [where she lives and grew up, born to Iranian parents] recently and I convinced her not only to allow us to show her work but also to come to Nepal."

Setting up the photofestival has been a gradual process. Building on the momentum of Photo.Circle, they identified an urgent need for context for their activities, and were inspired by the work of Shahidul Alam in Bangladesh

(still in prison as we went to press, after being arrested for making critical remarks about the government) who'd set up the Chobi Mela festival that Kakshapati first visited in 2009. "Through building a small community and organising a number of events in those early years, it became clear that there was no recorded history of Nepali photography, so this became an early focus for us," she says. Out of this, the Nepal Picture Library was born in 2011, which began to earnestly collect and digitise the images of older photographers whose work was in danger of being lost. To date, the library has collected more than 70,000 photographs from various private and organisational sources across Nepal, and the focus has always remained clear: "We were determined that the library be a multicultural and pluralist repository of Nepali history."

The first photographer they collaborated with was Mukunda Bahadur Shrestha, who'd been employed by the government for more than 35 years to travel around the country. "Like many other photographers in that period, he'd been tasked with creating the picturesque image synonymous with Nepal that

international audiences are used to seeing. The work he made on behalf of the government ended up as postcards, posters, calendars and so on to be sold to tourists. His remit was to make Nepal look like Shangri-La! We spent two years archiving his work – more than 11,000 images – and as we dug deeper, we found that none of his work has been collected or retained by the government department he had been working for. We had to find the original negatives and prints under his bed, in his closet, and in storage at his children's houses. There was an urgency with him, and with subsequent other photographers we worked with, as they were no longer young. Luckily in this case we were able to organise an exhibition of Shrestha's work just a few months before he passed away, so he was able to see the outcome of all his, and our, hard work."

The Nepal Picture Library has now successfully digitised the work of dozens of Nepali photographers, and as it has grown has been able to draw on a wider range of volunteers with experience in art history, preservation, archiving and cultural histories. One tangible result of this effort is highlighted

3

constantly thinking about nuance," she says. "Our local audiences engage with the festival in a big way, and they will challenge us if they can't relate to the work."

There was no better example of this spirit than in April 2015, when an earthquake hit Kathmandu in the build-up to the first festival. The preparations halted and the festival team downed tools to work on earthquake relief. Following a challenging period without fuel and other basic services, the festival team analysed the picture of Nepal that was being projected out into the world and it clarified their purpose. "We were very aware that this picture of destruction had gone out, and that this would have a serious impact on the tourism industry. We were emboldened to go ahead with the festival and we were determined to present an image of Nepal to the world to counter the mainstream media's sweeping generalisations of what was going on." Kishor Sharma, photographer and member of the festival's core organising team remembers this time as a defining moment. "Patan is an ancient and historic part of Kathmandu and was heavily affected by the earthquake. The festival helped to reconstruct the community in different ways. We kept all the visiting artists and visitors in local hotels, and they were able to interact easily with the locals. The locating of the festival in Patan helped local businesses in a small way."

This first edition featured only Nepalis, or international photographers who had been working in Nepal on long-form projects (such as Kevin Bubriski and Philip Blenkinsop), and was a way to show this work about Nepal in Nepal to a local audience for the first time. The second edition spread its net wider while still remaining true to the festival's original intentions, with the inclusion of work from Asia and beyond. One of the feature shows was Tasneem Alsultan's *Saudi Tales of Love* [5], which was able to engage the local audience in a very specific and intentional way. Kakshapati tells me that Saudi Arabia is the number one foreign destination for Nepali migrant workers, and that Saudi has received a justifiably bad rap in recent times. "Nepali workers are notoriously badly treated in Saudi, especially women. Many people here have family members working in Saudi, and Tasneem's work allowed us to really see another side to this place we all know so well but have not visited." Alsultan, who visited the festival in 2016 and took part in a number of different discussion panels and events, reflects on her experiences there. "My work was printed and displayed on the streets, and people walking past would stop and read the captions. I loved seeing how the locals had the opportunity to participate and engage with

in a feature exhibition in this year's festival, *The Feminist Memory Project* [3]. This initiative started only five months ago, after the Nepal Picture Library received a Magnum Foundation grant to unearth material that could be used to visualise the history of the women's rights movement in Nepal through photographs, letters, journals, diary entries, objects, documents, legal case files, songs, poems, oral histories and illustrations. *The Feminist Memory Project* is the first of its kind in the region and sets out to lay down these narratives via these aides-mémoire. It is a vital project at this time in Kathmandu's history, says Kakshapati: "The exhibition will focus

particularly on the public lives of women, and 'publicness' in general within the context of the feminist movement. The works will be installed in a highly visible public venue – Patan Durbar Square. *The Feminist Memory Project* will continue to grow beyond Photo Kathmandu. We hope to engage further with all the incredible content we are unearthing, to create books and other publications, conversations, learning tools that we want to develop for Nepali students and teachers, and maybe one day a film."

Kapashapati and her team are clear that they are accountable to the local Nepali population, and understand that they must show work that their audience can relate to. "We are

wider and deeper than just these few weeks. The festival allows us to create visibility for all the other things we do, and allows us to create opportunities for exchange in the future."

This year, says Kakshapati, promises to be a memorable event. "We are constantly thinking about ways to improve the quality of the exhibitions and events. We are also ramping up the public programming this year." The schedule is firmly focused on adding to the wider recognition of the importance of photography, and includes a number of tours and events specially designed for local school and college groups, as well as seminars and workshops exclusively for local teachers. A case in point is an ambitious project with Indian filmmaker and artist Amar Kanwar, *The Lightning Testimonies*, an eight-channel video piece that tackles the theme of sexual violence within conflict situations in the subcontinent. Alongside the video installation will be six full months of programming exploring the topic, and connecting this work back to the powerful *Feminist Memory Project* exhibiting in an adjacent space.

"I have participated or helped in every festival," says Sharma, summing up its value neatly as "a platform to learn, share and to engage with quality work from around the globe". For Hura, the Indian photographer who has been a collaborator since the early days of Photo.Circle, long before he was invited to join Magnum Photos, it's the comradeship of the growing team, the ethos of nurturing local talent and the festival's humble roots. "It's beautiful how all of them have not only started to take forward the idea of a community that had been dreamed of so many years ago, but have also come into their own as photographers," he says, having just set foot back in Nepal to teach another workshop. "What I see of Photo Kathmandu today is nothing but an extension of those lovely warm nights on the office terrace where they would screen projections on the neighbours' walls after they had fallen asleep – only the family has now gotten bigger." **BJP**

photoktm.com

the work. Kathmandu is one of my favourite festivals. Some locals stopped me to tell me they were glad to have their perception of Saudi women changed, and that they could connect with Saudi culture in a way they didn't think possible."

This year, Photo Kathmandu has 14 exhibitions, running alongside a series of residencies and workshops staged by a team of international photographers that includes Katrin Koenning, Robin Hammond, Sumit Dayal, Pablo Bartholomew and the Bombay Flying Club collective, as well as Valentina Abenavoli, one half of the team behind Akina Books, who will be undertaking a mixed-media residency for four weeks, collaborating with writer and editor Ilgin Deniz Akseloglu from Turkey. All this activity aside, the festival team is still relatively small and, as is true

for most festivals in this part of the world, the budget is incredibly tight, spread thinly across the programming, and is dependent on the participating artists being open to collaboration and being flexible when it comes to installing their exhibitions in venues around Patan and Kathmandu.

"We are constantly discussing how to manage this thing we have created, and asking ourselves why are we doing this," Kakshapati tells me. "Our discussions always come back to our community in Nepal, and the positive effect it has here. It has been heartening but scary to see that the word gets out internationally about what we are doing, and it puts a strange pressure on us. However, we've come to the conclusion that the festival is just the tip of the iceberg of what we do here. The activities and projects we have spread far

Next issue
November 2018

Patrick Waterhouse is best known for his collaborative practice, creating a series of Survival Guides as editor of *Colors* magazine, and partnering with Mikhael Subotzky on the Deutsche Börse-winning *Ponte City*. We visit him at his London studio to see his latest work, made with the Warlpiri of central Australia, discussing how he approached the sensitive subject of representing Aboriginal peoples. And with Paris Photo on the horizon, we highlight what's on show in the French capital, speaking to curator Martha Kirszenbaum about Curiosa, the fair's latest programme.

On sale 03 October

Looking for Honey Ants, with Julie Nangala Robertson,
from *Restricted Images: Made with the Warlpiri of Central Australia*
© Patrick Waterhouse, courtesy of SPBH Editions, 2018.

British Journal
of Photography

Creative Brief
Emily Keegin

Asked to describe the style of photography featured in *The Fader*, the celebrated music journal launched in New York in 1999 championing contemporary style and emerging artists, Keegin shoots back with, "All-you-can-eat buffet". The magazine's photo director since 2015, having previously worked for *Time* and *Bloomberg Businessweek*, she describes her preferred aesthetic as "manic", explaining, "I like all kinds of photography and am happiest when genre, style and hue smash into each other on the same page".

While her predecessors championed intimacy and authenticity, gaining unusual access to musicians and shooting them in relaxed pose in natural light, Keegin's approach injects flash, colour and surrealism. "To me, great photography is the result of an emotional connection between a photographer and her subject," she says. "This form of interpersonal magic is not genre specific or the result of a certain set of aesthetic constraints."

Is access still the watchword?
The music industry has changed since we began. Today, getting a musician to commit to unlimited multi-day access, with no hair and makeup, is unusual. Cover shoots tend to be two days long: one where we focus on portraits and cover concepts, followed by a day – or two – spent with the artist documenting their life.

Are you conscious of music clichés?
We used to avoid them by photographing all musicians at home, away from the studio and the trappings of cheesy guitar shots. This resulted in a lot of them being photographed in bed – which became its own *Fader* cliché. I'm less strict than my predecessors. I actually like seeing artists working in their studio, and it can bring an extra dimension to a story. The biggest portrait cliché I want to crush is the pouty/sad/mouth open/no expression/looking-off-into-the-distance face. I hate this. Humans have emotions, damn it! Faces are only interesting if they are expressive. My creative direction often asks the photographer to push for a range of expressions and gestures, and to "embrace art, light, creativity and life". Eye contact is great. I also have a set of no's. No chain-link fences. No prayer hands. No posing with an instrument. No singing into a mic with eyes closed.

Your thoughts on established photographers versus young talent?
I've had shoots with established photographers where the subject has walked off the set. And I've had shoots with emerging photographers where the subject vibed and granted them unprecedented access. From what I can tell, the only real difference between new and established photographers is how easily they are able to manage production and workflow. The biggest issue I've found with young photographers is shoddy post-production and an inability to correctly process files on deadline. While tremendously unsexy, being able to deliver on time is a critical part of the job. Often I will assign young photographers a number of smaller shoots to help teach them the ropes.

Name a project that you particularly enjoyed working on.
Jason Nocito on the Ariana Grande cover story [2]. Jason takes creative direction and spins it into something highly personal, artful and subtly surreal. For this cover, I was very keen on an 'American Kodak' feel. I sent Jason many Christopher Williams and Roe Ethridge reference images, swatches of gingham fabric, and I droned on about the lemon tree outside my office window. He held onto this direction and gave it a pulse. For big pop-star shoots, I like working with photographers I can trust to shoulder production, direct crowds and work quickly. Jason has the ability to do all the technical stuff without losing his desire for weird. He is an even-keeled maniac genius. His photographs show this. **BJP**

thefader.com/magazine

Portrait © Emily Keegin.

1   *Butt* (*What a Butt Wants* fashion feature) © Caroline Tompkins.

2   Ariana Grande, for the Summer 2018 issue © Jason Nocito.

3   Sampha, for the Summer Music Issue, June/July 2016 © Francesco Nazardo.

4   Lil Uzi Vert, for The Sex Issue, March/April 2017 © Tyler Mitchell.

5   Yaeji © David Brandon Geeting.

1

2

3

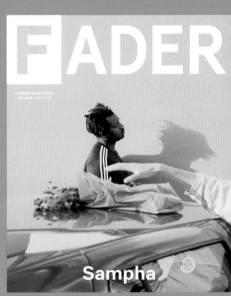

FADER

SUMMER MUSIC ISSUE
104 JUNE/JULY 2016

Sampha

5

4

FADER

Lil Uzi Vert

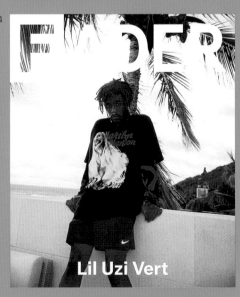

Huawei P20 Pro and Samsung Galaxy S9+

With smartphone camera spec advancing at pace, Damien Demolder sees how two of the most prominent fare in the professional sphere

Not many professional photographers buy a smartphone with the intention of using its camera for their work, but I expect there are plenty of times that professional photographers wish the camera on their phone took better pictures. We can't have all our kit with us all the time and there are occasions where we might want to blend in to avoid changing the situation. On these occasions a reliable smartphone camera that takes high-quality images would really pay off.

Reasonable cameraphones have been around for a while, but have often failed to offer a number of critical tools, such as focal-length choices, aperture controls, decent detail gathering and good quality in low light. Fortunately, smartphone technology moves much quicker than that in proper cameras, and progress is being made to address many of these shortcomings – both with hardware and sometimes with processing, or 'artificial intelligence'.

Recent models that appear to have made significant steps include the Samsung Galaxy S9+ and the Huawei P20 Pro, but how close to

a proper camera's output these smartphones can ultimately get remains to be seen.

The 40MP monster

A smartphone that offers 40MP resolution is bound to get our attention, but it is the choice of three camera/sensor combinations and some advanced AI that make the Huawei P20 Pro so interesting. We've seen equally high-resolution phone sensors in the past, but models such as Nokia's 41MP Lumia 1020 and 808 PureView used much smaller sensors. This model uses one that is about twice the size of that in standard smartphones and it collects about 20 per cent more light, despite its slower-than-average f/2.4 aperture.

This main 40MP sensor can record DNG raw files as well as JPEGs, and each image measures 7280×5456 pixels. If you take 300ppi to be the standard for 'photo quality' printing that gives you an image size of just over 24×18in. The raw files are 76MB, but are only 10-bit so we cannot expect the dynamic range of a raw file from a regular camera – but it should be better than that from a standard 8-bit JPEG and

us to drop from a potential 40MP to just 10. But the quality of images shot through the longer lens is better than shooting at 40MP and cropping to match the angle of view – that just gives you a five-million pixel image.

Depth-of-field features

Wide lenses – such as those on small sensor devices like phones – tend to offer extensive depth-of-field and little opportunity to use differential focusing to lift a subject from a background, even though some have very wide apertures. It is physics that determines the depth-of-field for any lens/aperture/subject distance combination, but these smartphones attempt to bypass the science to create background blur for creative effect. The Galaxy S9+ achieves this through the use of two physical apertures, one of f/2.4 and the other of f/1.5. Obviously, the wider aperture presents a shallower depth-of-field – though in practice there isn't much difference and f/1.5 produces a less-sharp image. Panasonic also used a physical aperture in its Lumix DMC-CM1 and offered a range from f/2.8 to f/11, but even with its larger 1in sensor the aperture served to control the flow of light rather than determine the depth-of-field.

Samsung enhances the depth-of-field effect with internal software that identifies the subject and then blurs the background, with varying degrees of success. It experiences some difficulty detaching hair and edges from the background, so often the results don't stand up to scrutiny.

The P20 Pro uses a method based around its AI. Using the monochrome sensor to provide distance information it is able to determine which parts of the image are close and which are distant, and thus which should be sharp and which soft. It then adds degrees of blur accordingly. Working this way, the camera can add blur more selectively, and to objects in front of, as well as behind the subject, so the overall effect is more convincing. Out-of-focus highlights in the background are rendered perfectly round, as if a £2000 lens has been used, but even though it does a better job than the S9+, not all stray details are dealt with well. The laws of physics are difficult to change, but in some cases this software blurring can be effective.

much better than a usual smartphone is able to achieve.

The resolution that results from this sensor and the Leica lens in front of it is pretty surprising. The pair collect masses of detail, and images are sharp across the frame with even corner information well presented. Dynamic range is very good too – better than it should be – so when we shoot in raw we can create detailed images with the appearance of moderate contrast. Image files are pretty flexible in Adobe Camera Raw and will withstand a good degree of pulling around without the tonal transitions breaking apart. It is all very impressive – and genuinely useful.

The P20 Pro's second camera uses a monochromatic sensor that is, of course, very good for black-and-white. This camera has 20 million pixels and only shoots in JPEG mode, but because all the pixels record in black-and-white we get one-to-one processing and exceptional detail. The dynamic range is a bit short, but generally the images look very nice – though I'd still prefer to shoot colour in raw and process to monochrome afterwards.

Multiple focal lengths

Smartphones are usually restricted to wide-angle lenses and we have to shoot everything with a 28mm-style focal length. This means that what we can use them for is also restricted unless we are happy to endure the perspective exaggeration of working close-up. The Galaxy S9+ and P20 Pro offer the usual wide focal length on one camera, but both have an extra longer lens on an additional sensor. In the S9+ that secondary lens is the equivalent of a 52mm standard lens, while the P20 Pro's is more like an 80mm. Both cameras allow users to select these secondary lenses to achieve the longer focal length, and while the S9+ offers a 12MP sensor behind both cameras, the P20 Pro drops to 10MP output when the 80mm lens is used – and it can't shoot in raw.

If you can cope with the lower resolution – and 10/12 million pixels still gives a 12×9/13×10in print – these longer focal lengths are useful. With the S9+ there's no resolution penalty for using it, as both lenses have the same 12MP-type sensor behind them. The P20 Pro, however, forces

Decisive moments are not easily achieved with either camera, with both requiring the user to become accustomed to typical lag times and to anticipate the moment more than usual. The Samsung Galaxy S9+ (left) is better in this regard and has slightly quicker and regular reactions, but the Huawei P20 Pro (right) rewards us with better dynamic range and more detail once we master its ways.

Working in low light

Small sensors and small pixels are not conducive to clean images in low light. Some noise every now and then is harmless, even enjoyable, especially for those with an appreciation for the film era, but when digital noise destroys detail and processing tries to make up for it, we can end up with an unusable mess.

Both these cameras use some form of trickery to get the best out of low-light situations and both do a remarkably good job of it. Even without a tripod, multiple exposures are combined and aligned in processing to marry extra luminance information with chromatic recordings to create clean-ish images with reasonably well-saturated colours. The Galaxy S9+ has the advantage of a f/1.5 maximum aperture matched with optical image stabilisation to keep the ISO down and the camera-shake at bay, while the P20 Pro has the advantage of a larger sensor that has more pixels to down-sample to improve the final 10-megapixel image.

The multiple exposure techniques allow something of an HDR effect, as well as low noise levels, even when the ISO has to ramp up. Particularly impressive is both cameras' ability to compensate for handheld work with long exposures by realigning the multiple exposures in-camera before output. In extreme cases, this doesn't work out, and if you have someone walking in the frame they may end up with three or four legs, but on the whole, if you attempt to hold the camera still, you will get decent results.

What they lack

The greatest weakness of these cameras is the delay between asking them to take a picture and them actually doing so. In many cases this won't matter and most users will not notice, but if you are trying to time a moving subject so you can get it in exactly the right place, these cameras will prove a challenge. The Galaxy S9+ reacts quickest and is fairly good when used in normal, bright conditions, but it took me a long time to get used to the degree of anticipation required to get the P20 Pro to record the moment I wanted. In Pro mode, which you might – fairly – expect to be the most responsive, there is a significant delay after the button press before the image is recorded, so I found myself judging the time and shooting a little early. Fortunately the delay is consistent, so if you have the opportunity to practise you can learn to take account of it. Switched into Auto mode, though, the camera seems to record before the shutter is pressed, so I found myself in the odd position of waiting for the subject to have gone beyond the spot before I pressed the button. Either way, neither model reacts like a DSLR or a mirrorless camera, and will be a frustration to those for whom timing is critical. Nevertheless, the high drive modes of both models are impressive, so if you can live without any control over exposure and the like, that will be the answer.

The second aspect that most will find frustrating is that both models are made for people who may only take the occasional picture, making shooting decisions for each shot. This means the carefully selected options that we might choose to work with all the time are forgotten every time the camera function is shut down. Simple stuff, such as white balance, has to be set each time you switch between modes, as it defaults to AWB whenever it gets the chance. ISO settings also drop off. Perhaps it is something to get used to, but these little things become big things when you are out in the field and will slow

From the Samsung (left) and Huawei images (right), we can see that both models offer decent controls over focusing and metering, with exposure compensation and metering linked to the AF area. Favourite settings tend not to be remembered though, which can be frustrating, and things like white balance slip back to auto when you least expect it. Illustrative images © Damien Demolder.

everything down. It is issues such as these that indicate these are not products geared for professionals, but rather for those who prefer to shoot in auto.

This is once again reinforced by the fact that they are both made of glass, front and back. Although this means they are elegant to look at, it also makes them fragile. The silky finish of the back panels are frictionless, making both cameras prone to sliding off any smooth surface you put them down on. Rubber-armoured cases will be required to prevent the deadly shattering of corners and screens.

Conclusions

As we might expect, these cameraphones are good at some things and not so good at others. Of the two models, I much prefer the Huawei P20 Pro – purely for its 40MP mode and the quality of image it can produce. The appeal of this is in the traditional characteristics by which we judge cameras – the sharpness and details of the images they produce, and the dynamic range. On each of these points, it scores very well, and its performance in good conditions means it can certainly be used for high-quality work.

> **"The artificial intelligence does help elevate these models to a level of utility that we might not expect from a smartphone, but it is a poor substitute for what most of us require for professional images"**

The artificial intelligence does help elevate these models to a level of utility that we might not expect from a smartphone, but it is, in the main, a poor substitute for what most of us require for professional images. The blurred backgrounds and foregrounds created by the Huawei model are more subtle and convincing than those generated artificially by the Samsung one, but the latter can get part of the way there without software, instead using its wider maximum aperture.

In all, these are both good cameras and there are certainly applications in professional life for them both. The Huawei P20 Pro is a number of steps ahead in terms of the image quality it can provide in its Pro mode and with 'raw' activated. When the situation arises in which you find you don't want to carry a proper camera, this handy substitute will do a number of jobs very well. I am rather taken with what it can do and impressed with its quality. If I had a project to shoot portraits of people somewhere I didn't want to stand out as a photographer, I'd be very glad to use it and would be confident of the results. **BJP**

huawei.com/uk
samsung.com/uk

Follow us on social media:

city lit

Photo: **E Jean Johnson Jones**
Parkour Leap

A small selection of Autumn courses in Central London

Essential business skills for photographers
VY988 Mon 01 Oct - 15 Oct, 18:00 -21.00

City Lit Pro: Adobe Lightroom intensive
VY987 Fri 05 Oct- 26 Oct, 18.00-21.15

Documentary photography and photojournalism
VY600 Mon 08 Oct - 10 Dec, 10.00-13.00

Photography discussion group with Shirley Read
VY975 Tues 09 Oct - 06 Nov, 18.30-20.30

City Lit photography long course
VY844 Wed 10 Oct - 20 Mar, 10.00-17.00

Close-up photography
VY745 Thur 11 Oct - 08 Nov, 18.00-21.00

Photography for beginners with Adobe Lightroom
VY718 Wed 17 Oct - 05 Dec, 18.30-21.30

City Lit Pro: event photography
VY948 Mon 22 Oct - 12 Nov, 18.15-21.30

Nature photography day out: London Parks in Autumn
VY424 Sat 27 Oct, 10.00-16.00

Photograph City of London architecture
VY949 Tues 30 Oct - 20 Nov, 14.00-17.00

Follow us on Twitter @CityLitArts

Our studios in Covent Garden have up-to-date equipment and offer a comfortable and inspiring learning experience. To enrol now or for a comprehensive view of all our courses please visit:
www.citylit.ac.uk/BJP or call enrolments on **020 7831 7831**
1-10 Keeley Street, Covent Garden, London WC2B 4BA

Many a small thing has been made large by the right kind of advertising.
Mark Twain

To advertise here please contact
+44 (0)20 7193 6763

British Journal of Photography

Endframe
The Black Image Corporation

Words by Alice Zoo

The archives of two stellar magazines who championed black women ahead of their time are opened up in Milan

Image © Isaac Sutton, courtesy of Johnson Publishing Company, LLC.

"There were things happening in black America that lend themselves to the conversation in Italy in a way that perhaps people never would have imagined," says Theaster Gates, a social practice artist and curator of a new exhibition, *The Black Image Corporation*, dedicated to exploring the legacy of the Johnson Publishing Company archive and its two acclaimed magazines, *Ebony* and *Jet*.

Presented at the Fondazione Prada from 20 September to 14 January, the exhibition gathers photographs from the company's extensive archive of more than four million images, focusing primarily on the work of two photographers, Moneta Sleet Jr and Isaac Sutton. "When the Prada Foundation invites you to do a project, you know there's already this big and ambitious living legacy; and so it felt really amazing to then put the Johnson Publishing Company in the context of this other fashion family," explains Gates.

Ebony and *Jet* magazines, published from 1945 onwards, were aimed at African-American audiences, reflecting the mid-century aesthetic in the US, but with a lens specifically focused on black life. Against the flow of negative or stereotypical depictions of black women that had preceded it, "*Ebony* committed itself to celebrating black women. This is before black women were on the covers of *Vogue,* so 30 or 40 years before the mainstream world was ready to see a black image in the most positive sense, there was already this corporation that had the ideology and financial muscle to celebrate black women," says Gates. *The Black Image Corporation* explores these magazines' extraordinary legacy, presenting their images – everyday candid photographs of mothers

and working women alongside actresses and models – together, setting the under-represented beauty of black American life in postwar USA into a gallery context.

Built as a structure reflecting on an architectural form called a studiolo – a small room dedicated to the storage and display of art – the exhibition's participatory element is crucial. Visitors will have the opportunity to pull prints out of cabinets and display them themselves, creating an ever-changing and self-developing show. In addition to the display of prints, visitors will have access to hundreds of issues of *Ebony* and *Jet* magazines, allowing them to peruse the full gamut of the archives in situ. This participation will cast the viewer into the same curatorial role as the editors of the magazines: reflecting on, presenting, and foregrounding images. "I think that when people are allowed into the artistic process, they leave those situations with a more thorough understanding, not only of the

artistic device, but they start to see the subject in new ways," says Gates.

The exhibition's opening coincides with Milan Fashion Week, and Gates, an artist known for his interest in bringing cultures together, notes the significance of the overlap. "It's a tool of image education as much as it is a celebration of something artistic," he explains, although he hopes that any visitor to the Fondazione's Osservatorio "would first walk in and be stunned by beauty".

Perhaps Fashion Week audiences might come upon the show and reflect on the deficit of mainstream images celebrating the beauty of black women in the 1940s and 1950s. "These archives investigate the themes of beauty and black female power, and I think today is the right time to dig into the visual lexicon of American history and unveil an iconography that, outside of my community, enjoys poor visibility," states Gates. **BJP**

fondazioneprada.org